John Bascom

Comparative Psychology

The growth and grades of intelligence

John Bascom

Comparative Psychology
The growth and grades of intelligence

ISBN/EAN: 9783337368432

Printed in Europe, USA, Canada, Australia, Japan

Cover: Foto ©Thomas Meinert / pixelio.de

More available books at **www.hansebooks.com**

COMPARATIVE PSYCHOLOGY

OR,

THE GROWTH AND GRADES OF INTELLIGENCE.

BY

JOHN BASCOM,

Author of Philosophy of Religion, Principles of Psychology, Philosophy of English Literature, etc.

NEW YORK:

G. P. PUTNAM'S SONS,

182 FIFTH AVE.

1878.

PREFACE.

THE advocates of the Empirical Philosophy are wont to criticise the Intuitional Philosophy in two respects ; first, as overlooking the relation between the mature mind and the mind of the infant, between rudimentary and developed powers ; and, second, as overlooking the still more important connection between the intelligence of to-day and that of remote previous periods, between the intelligence of man and that of animals, and of the earlier human life from which it has been derived. We grant these points to be well taken, especially the latter. Without tracing the history of intelligence, we are not prepared to decide what is primitive and what is acquired, what is original material and what is the deposit of growth. The empiricist cannot be fully and fairly met without traveling with him these spaces of evolution, and determining at least their general facts and laws. This I have undertaken in the present volume. It is my purpose to test the nature and extent of the modifications put upon human psychology by its relations in growth to the life below it, and in doing this to reach a general statement of each stage of development.

Many results of such an inquiry must be partial, and many conjectural ; and still they are sufficient, it seems to me, to enable us to decide with some certainty on the general value of the accepted doctrines of the Intuitional Philosophy. At all events, the chosen ground on which the Empirical Philosophy has set the battle in order is accepted, and the conflict joined. Notwithstanding the bellicose image, I trust the inquiry has been ordered in an open-handed way, and that due consideration has been given to all opposing facts. I have derived great benefit from many forms of Empirical Philosophy ; these I cheerfully acknowledge, while I must remain its unflinching adversary. The Intuitional Philosophy can and should appropriate these excellent fruits, and this volume is the result of such an effort. Its subject, the Growth and Grades of Intelligence, would hardly have been suggested but for the Empirical Philosophy, nor could the discussion have been carried on without it. We gladly accept the many truths which this philosophy furnishes, but we build them into an edifice very different from that for which they were quarried.

CONTENTS.

INTRODUCTION.

METAPHYSICS, by which we understand an inquiry into mental facts as something after and beyond physical facts, has suffered in our time greater disparagement than any other branch of knowledge. Contempt has been joined to aversion, and the two have found expression much at random. If any discussion becomes peculiarly verbal, or any inquiry particularly subtle, it is at once spoken of as metaphysical. Yet no researches are more legitimate, none more unavoidable, none more fruitful than those of metaphysics or philosophy. Metaphysics can only be attacked with arrows taken from its own quiver, and their flint-heads are one truth or another whose grounds of assertion are to be found in the laws of the mind. The sweep of these discussions is as broad as religious and social activity, and their value will remain pre-eminent, unless we are to reach a day in which the raiment shall be more than the body it clothes, and meat more than the life it feeds.

This dissatisfaction, however, with metaphysics has its advantages. It has led to a careful sifting of its methods of inquiry, and to an effort to supplement them by physical researches. This effort has gone in fact much farther, and has aimed to displace mental by physical facts, and to substitute investigations in matter for those in mind. Yet the ephah of barley it brings home from its extended gleanings is after all the clear recognition of certain physical inquiries as valuable adjuncts to those of philosophy.

The two directions in which this fact is more manifest are, first, the construction and functions of the human brain ; and, second, the physical and psychical steps of progress in the animal kingdom by which the pre-eminence of man may be said to have been reached. The two are included in comparative psychology.

By comparative psychology we understand a knowledge of intelligence, of conscious activity, as it exists in all accessible forms of lives, a tracing of its development in its several stages through the entire animal kingdom. This is our present effort, a discussion of the growth and grades of intelligence in the world about us. We need, in this inquiry, not only to understand, as well as we may, each form of conscious activity, but its immediate nervous conditions, the lower vital and atomic powers on which these are superinduced, and the slow increments one upon another, by which all is finally built up into the composite mind of man, the crowning spiritual structure of the world ; which some hold to have come down from Heaven, and some to have sprung from the earth, but which we are ready to believe has, rather, like every living thing, been ministered to by each seen and unseen agent, and taken into itself the strength of both realms.

If this work is successfully done, we shall understand our faculties in the analysis which time, which evolution, has given them. The actual growth of the mind from its own historic germs will be before us; powers will be seen in their dependencies, and we shall be able to correct our previous analysis by that discrimination and separation of elements which have attended on their constructive introduction. Much may be done by such inquiry to confirm, modify and correct our philosophy, though philosophy is, after all, its own necessary antecedent, the light in which its comprehending powers go on.

In entering on this labor there are peculiar dangers, dangers which arise from a philosophy too defective safely to discuss its own problems in their more remote and obscure forms. Wisdom is the condition of wisdom, and this the more manifestly as we traverse regions thinly sown with supersensual truths. In tracing the growth of intelligence we necessarily start with purely physical forces; this has been the order of evolution and it must be of inquiry. Our first danger, therefore, is, that we shall be unwilling to enlarge our principles so as to include the new facts, we may meet, without distortion or mutilation. The action of causation applies strictly to local, atomic forces; here, and here only, does the law of the equivalence of forces find room. If we reason from it as if it existed elsewhere, without first establishing its existence, and the precise form of it, we are sure to be misled. If we have pre-determined that our explanations must express every new fact, like every old one, in terms of mat-ter and motion, we at once preclude all increments, and growth sinks with us into a rolling over of our first facts, a rigid development of our primary prem-ises. The problems of life, of intelligence, of spir-itual powers, as they arise in order, are forced down in their solution under laws and conceptions made for them in matter, not found for them in mind. Our explanations no longer explain, for they so alter and reduce the phenomena, put atomic forces to such strange and extravagant service, that there is no known relation between our facts and our theories, between the apparent effects and the causes assigned them. This is a fundamental danger. The mind does not rise from the lower to the higher but merges the higher in the lower. It loses one of the two terms of the problems, and so misconceives them both.

A second danger is, that we shall infer from a similarity of external appearances an equivalence of internal conscious states, though the two sets of facts are found on very different planes of life. Thus on the ground of some resemblance of actions we enrich the mind of the animal with the thoughts and affections which belong to man, forgetful that each increment of intelligence permeates downward, and modifies all below it. Lower activities take place in man under the light of a much more clear and extended consciousness than do corresponding states

in the animal, and are therefore by no means identical with these even when primarily referable to
the same faculties. Each being is organically harmonious, is complete within itself. The increments
which belong to it, as compared with one lower, are
not detached, a certain something on the surface of
its being; but are interwoven in mutual modifications with all its other powers. The higher gifts
especially must be allowed their freedom in acting
on and modifying the lower ones. This fact cuts
us off from the easy inference, that certain faculties always carry with them like, or proximately
like, states of consciousness, since the associated
conditions of their exercise may greatly alter the results. As we pass up in intelligence we are especially to recollect that what has been given us at previous stages is now shaped by the pressure of quite
different powers, debarring us from the conclusion
that present states of consciousness correspond
with any exactness to former ones. Precisely the
opposite inference is in order, and each form of life
must be admitted to the thoughts in its own new-
ness and organic completeness.

A farther danger is, that we shall not enter
on our inquiry in full possession of all that belongs to us, all that is necessary to make it successful. Idealists have created a great deal of
worthless metaphysics by saying to themselves,—
What is that one most certain thing from which
we can start in establishing all other things?
What is the single simple idea from which every
other idea can be derived? Such inquiries are

sure to result in the thinnest filaments of thought, the lightest web of speculation floating high above the facts to which it has at most a single point of attachment. It is lost to the eye in all ordinary light, and only comes forth when some peculiarly favoring ray falls upon it.

Why should I take the notion of being as primary, and see what can be derived from it, when I have other notions and other impressions equally independent, equally primary, equally constructive? Such a method removes its conclusions at every step more and more from the facts, when the only value of any method lies in the correspondence of facts and conclusions.

The materialist in his own way does the same thing when he takes a physical relation, enlarges it in statement, and spreads its terms over phenomena intrinsically opposed to it. He too falls into word-building. He too is unwilling to take starting-points in their integrity.

Our inquiries should rather be, What and how much can I rightfully, qualifiedly assume? How much is contained in the phenomena? How much do my combined faculties give me? All our faculties stand on the same footing of authority, and it is irrational to take their data in part, and reject them in part. And, as intuitive faculties necessarily give phenomena distinct and primitive in character, it follows at once that no logical process will deduce the facts of one set of faculties successfully from those of another. We can not reason from sight to sound, from touch to taste, from experience to rational intuition. What is primitive we must accept in a primitive way, or miss it altogether. Nothing is plainer than this ; if we have a right to the use of one limb we have a right to the use of both ; if I am wise in using one I am still wiser in using both. The metaphysician, when he insists on selecting one truth as self-evident and seeing what can be done under these narrow conditions, is no more a master in his art than the poet who measured his abilities by seeing the number of lines he could write standing on one foot.

When the scientist inquires into material facts, he adopts our method. He assumes the action of the senses, the intuitive and reflective powers involved, and then proceeds with his investigation. We should do the same in psychology. We should accept our mental faculties completely for what they ostensibly are, and then push forward our researches. If our labors issue in a new analysis, a new reference of powers, very well ; but we have no right by anticipation to disparage any power, or to insist on its secondary and derived character till this has been shown. A tacit or avowed philosophy accompanies our inquiries into philosophy, and this, our antecedent conviction, must be measurably complete and honest, or we shall be hopelessly misled by it. We cannot, in the outset, cripple our powers without thereby, in the end, marring our results. It is sound sense in all inquiries to hold fast what we have, or seem to have, till its value is fully tested; to carry with us to our work our best resources, and not to maim our movement by a skepticism so complete as to take away the very conditions of success. The physicist must, therefore, starting in the physical world for a long journey upward along the lines of evolution to the realms of mind, assume the existence of those faculties which he will need in every step of the route, and which can be to him his only guide either as to the direction or method of research. He who proposes to fight a loyal fight by stripping off his armor, will do no better than he who makes ready for battle by riveting it all on. Wisdom, not hair-brained heroism, not arrant cowardice, is our need. We are to hold firmly, and, on occasion, yield easily, what we have; equally careful in retention and in concession to let no advantage slip. A certain faith that can advance without hesitation and retreat without fear, in steady pursuit of the main purpose, is no less the condition of philosophy and of science, than of war.

CHAPTER I.

MIND AND MATTER.

As intelligence is seen in its primary manifestations, and still more in its antecedent conditions, to penetrate, in comparative psychology, far down among material forces, and, by the mediation of an automatic life, to be extensively interlaced with them, it is very desirable in opening our discussion to define the relations of mind and matter to each other. If we hold firmly apart these two centres of all our knowledge, we shall handle in analysis the more safely and intelligibly intervening phenomena. We shall not float from position to position with no sufficient recognition of the spaces passed over. This, then, is our first topic, the relation of mind and matter.

There is no division more incorporate into the experience of the entire race of man than that between mind and matter, thought and the external objects with which thought deals, arranging activity and a relatively inert material, subject to it. So true is this that to most persons any denial of this distinction as complete and radical is attended at once by that dimness of vision and obscurity of thought incident to dizziness and a sudden tremor running through all the lines of order. The few speculative minds who do obliter-

ate these fundamental divisions to which the common intelligence has all along conformed its work,
reach results so erratic, and so divergent one from
another, as to carry little belief, and to evoke hope-
less conflict. We must repose a certain faith in
the mind's primitive, spontaneous, constructive action, in its historic flow, as it plows its deep bed
along the decline of centuries, like great rivers
pressing seaward, or we shall lose all confidence in
its more brilliant, spasmodic efforts. Our philosophy must gather up the little with the large, the
ordinary with the extraordinary, the sluggish flow
onward and the sudden leap forward, the past with
the present, or the sense of security and truthful-
ness, of real forces registering real results every--
where, of an innate steadiness and growth of mind
which push it toward the light, will be lost. We
must pay at least this respect to the masses, to
remember that they furnish the facts which our
philosophy is to explain.

We may inquire into the separate conditions of
matter and mind, and the grounds of our belief in
them, but to raise the questions, Whether at bottom the facts of mind are not those of matter? or
those of matter those of mind? is to so subvert
intelligence in its primitive data as to force upon us
the painful conviction, we now know nothing, and it
is only too probable, therefore, that we shall never
know any thing. If all thought and experience
hitherto have crystallized along the dividing line
between mind and matter, have clustered about it
the fruits of knowledge, till it has become like a

rich vein stored with precious stones, and yet this line is now found quite fictitious, the insufficiency and insanity of our mental processes become so conspicuous as to take away all pleasure in farther effort. We must know, we must have known, something, and this too correctly, in order to make it worth while to inquire about any thing. That something is, for us at least, this first, fundamental division which pervades our rational life, that between mind and matter.

Mind is *non compos* if not correct in its initial action ; and what wisdom we have left should teach us, that the visions of lunatics are not worth pursuing. The mind must be lifted to its feet; must be able, in possession of itself, to survey the material world about it, before the gyrations of images can be orderly enough to remove dizziness from the brain itself.

The mind proceeds in all its acts of comprehension on certain fundamental antitheses, in which two things are held together, and made mutually to expound each other. The simplest product of thought, a judgment, is of this nature ; and the subject and the predicate support the proposition by a mutual explanation the one of the other. This antithesis, variable in form according to its uses, is that expressed in common language by the words, substance and qualities, agent and acts ; in science, by the words, cause and effect, force and phenomena ; in living things, by life and functions ; in psychology, by mind and faculties, noumena and phenomena ; in religion, by spirit and affections; in rhetoric, by thought and expression; in art, by substance and form; in the Universe at large, by plan and fulfilment, mind and matter, the thing shaping and the thing shaped, the free and the fixed. The fundamental contrast, in these opposites, that into which they chiefly fall in ultimate analysis, is that between mind and matter, the active and passive aspects of the constructive process. This antithetic structure and consideration of each topic are as essential to the progress of our thoughts as two limbs to the movement of our bodies. We swing from one to the other and so press forward. To leap on one leg is a difficult and desperate effort of which we soon tire; for the mind to attempt to handle one of these antithetic elements without the other is equally spasmodic and futile exertion. Reluctant as the Cosmic Philosophy, with its empirical tendencies, is to admit these fundamental distinctions of thought, and assign them their true position, it is compelled, in opposition to Positive Philosophy, to make this concession. "Not a step can be taken towards the truth, that our states of consciousness are the only things we can know, without tacitly or avowedly postulating an unknown something beyond consciousness. The proposition, that whatever we feel has an existence which is relative to ourselves only cannot be proved, nay, cannot even be intelligibly expressed without asserting, directly or by implication, an external existence which is not relative to ourselves." *

* Cosmic Philosophy, vol. i., p. 84.

This antithesis is fundamental in our constitution. It arises from what our senses and our intuitions respectively supply us ; while all thinking is the union of the two elements. If our avenues of knowledge were those of the senses simply, there would be present phenomena only, and these would flow on with no provocation of thought, no contrasts, no comparisons. But our intuitions bring to these the noumena, and instantly there spring up all the relations and dependencies of real being. The grounds of this double movement of thought are found in the divided physical and spiritual structure of man, in his perceptive and intuitive powers. It cannot, therefore, be escaped, or for a moment be deemed unsound.

The external and the internal worlds, matter and mind, are with us an ever-recognized distinction, lying at the very basis of all inquiry and all thought. We shall not for a moment efface a division which is the first line the mind draws in the construction of its chart of knowledge, a division so essential that, if we remove it, we must begin at once furtively to restore it, or all our distinctions, our comprehensive processes, flow together and are lost in unintelligible homogeneity.

The full recognition of mind in contrast with matter .involves, under human experience, two things : first, that mental processes are conscious processes, and these only ; second, that such processes beyond our own consciousness are adequately indicated to us by order, by the adaptation of means to ends. If thought is not thought, a conscious act ;

if the mind in its own activities is not always open to itself in its own light, then the analogies taken from our own experience are gone, and we know not what thought is, and may as well cease to discuss its nature. If arrangement and adjustment do not immediately or mediately express thought, are not, as opposed to un-adjustment, the products of mind, then again we have lost a first clue to knowledge as given by our own experience. White and black, sweet and sour, hot and cold, are no better distinctions than are these, order and disorder, plan and material, mind and matter, and no more pervade our practical activity.

There are two inquiries which we must make in all investigations, the means employed and the overruling idea. Without both, order, progress can not be explained. That certain something by which order is superior to disorder, and by which it is induced, is the gist of all knowledge. It is the product of the mind, and the sole delight of the mind. We accept these first truths, and so proceed to second truths. Our first truths in mind are, then, that mind is a spiritual power, that its phenomena are conscious states, that the external proof of these states are order, arrangement, coherent action.

When we turn to matter, the case is still simpler. We accept only forces—efficiencies—and phenomena; these phenomena themselves being effects in mind and relative to it. We must have mind and matter both, before we can have physical phenomena, since phenomena are nothing more nor less than the action of one on the other. We have causes and effects, forces and phenomena.

The mind can not be the forces, for these are only known to it by an inference which evokes them as agents independent of and antagonistic to itself. It can no more be the phenomena, for these have no existence save as we presuppose a mind to which they are addressed through the senses. The phenomena of matter are phenomena in and to mind alone, and thus presuppose mind. Any state of the brain incidental to sensation or thought can itself be known or conceived of only as phenomena recognized by the mind as external to itself, and can not, therefore, be mind. The external world or causes are more frequently spoken · of as of two kinds, matter and force. Force sufficiently well covers all the facts. There are fixed agencies known as matter, and mobile agencies known as forces, yet there would seem to be no fundamental distinction between the two. Matter is nothing more than the forces which produce its phenomena. This we must infer, and this is all that we are at liberty to infer. As we can not but put causes back of effects as broad as the effects, so we must not give the causes any breadth beyond the effects.

Moreover, the fixed forces expressed in matter are in flux with the motor forces. Heat is now locked up in the chemical affinities of atoms, affinities which determine the sensible properties of matter, and is now let loose again in mechanical motion. In the circle, within which forces correlate with each other, within which we can say no force is lost, fixed and motor forces draw on each other, and replace each other. The phenomenal, no matter how far we carry it, must ultimately disappear, and when it disappears, it can only leave that unphenomenal agency which is its source. Any effort to clothe this final force with material qualities is a confusion of thought ; a struggle to retain phenomena after we have theoretically passed beyond them. As, then, we ultimately reach force and this only, and as forces of both orders are interchangeable, force remains for us as the substratum of the material world. The fundamental contrast is force and phenomena, and as phenomena involve the presence of intellectual powers to receive them, it is that of matter and mind.

While force excludes mind, and is its one antithetic conception, it none the less has two elements, the second of which may show its emanation from mind. These elements are substance and form. Its form as precise, definite, adapted to an end, may declare its origin in mind. The numerical exactness of forces in their measurements, an exactness that becomes more obvious and complete as forces are more simple and primitive, indicates that they have emanated from mind, and received from mind one of its most full, peculiar and unmistakable impressions. What is a more indisputable product of mind than mathematics, its measurements, methods, curves, discussions ? And what in mathematics is more preëminently of the mind than its precision, its exact truths, its equalities ? Place any two stones a definite distance from each other,—cut a stick a given length, and mind is disclosed at once to all comers.

But the primitive forces of nature show the utmost precision in their action and combination ; they work under exhaustive mathematical formulæ. Gravitation, crystallization, chemical combination, the motion of light, heat, are all numerical ; and so arise out of order and work into order. These forces, therefore, in the precision of their activity, do the very highest that thought can do, answer exactly to thought, are open to the most perfect comprehension of thought, and give the only proof that can ever be given of springing from thought. It is the outlines and measurements of the pyramids that indicate their origin, that make but one supposition possible in reference to them.

But while matter, in its primitive forms and later combinations, includes that order which is the external language of mind to mind, it excludes mind as directly present in it. Mind is ever conscious, and mind only is conscious. This is our first truth, our point of departure. To speak of intelligence without consciousness is to cause to waver again our dividing line between matter and mind. Space and consciousness—there they stand as the fundamentally opposed forms of two orders of being. Forces occupy the one, mental activities the other, and in their interplay lies the whole field of knowledge.

We would not reiterate as we do these simple facts were they not so often, and in such various ways, overlooked, and with such ever-returning confusion. The moment explanation loses sight of the radical diversity between states of consciousness and any physical facts whatever, though they be states of brain, comprehension begins to be lost.

The boldest way in which this division is effaced is the direct assertion of the identity of the two activities involved in thought, that of the brain and that of the mind. Says Taine: "We are entitled then to admit that the cerebral event and the mental event are at foundation but one and the same event under two aspects, one moral, the other physical; one accessible to consciousness, the other accessible to the senses." *

This is to say, that a certain cerebral state knows itself, is conscious of itself, and this is thought. It also knows itself as it would appear to itself in vision, and as it would affect touch, and thus is prepared to say, that these sensational results and that intellectual result are the same thing, and its very self under different aspects; the views themselves being taken, and the comparison instituted by that which is the subject and object of them. It is impossible for confusion and incomprehensibility to go farther. A pure physical fact knows itself in consciousness, knows itself in sensation, perplexes itself because the two outlooks are not the same, and at length congratu-

* On Intelligence, p. 185.

lates itself in the brain of M. Taine because they are the same, and, more than that, its very self. Thus its words and distinctions, for a moment held apart as a condition of thought, are lost again in identity and thought disappears.

This conception cannot be constructed, cannot be held fast for an instant, if we really accept its conclusion, and identify the physical and mental facts. A simply physical fact cannot, without the addition of a transcendent power of some sort, erect itself above itself, and look at itself ; nay, secure two very different visions of itself, and then, collapsing into the center of its own circle of being, pronounce the whole movement and every part of it, the subject and the object, the seeing and the thing seen, the thinking and the thing thought, one simple and identical state. If any explanation was ever purely verbal, wholly alien to every form of experience, lifted into a moment's plausibility by the flitting images of the imagination, this is certainly it. We are not surprised to hear the same author explain mental processes in this wise: "The same image, becoming precisely situated, seems to be joined by its posterior extremity to the anterior extremity of the repressive images or sensations, and is thus joined to them." *

The anterior and posterior extremities of a thought, a desire, a volition ! Let us now talk of the smell of a rainbow, the harshness of a color, and the flavor of the wind. Yet these are the

* Ibid. p. 345.

men, breaking down all the divisions of experience, who none the less claim to draw their philosophy preëminently and exclusively from experience.

We would not so return to the various methods in which physical and mental phenomena are confounded and mutually confused, were it not that the philosophical and the scientific world are everywhere full of them, and that it is impossible to discuss satisfactorily the growth of intelligence without sweeping away these innumerable supposititious facts that have gathered about the mind. A physical image, with most psychologists, is a sufficient basis on which to assert a fact and construct a theory.

A less flagrant violation of the first term of experience, the separation of matter and mind, is the extension of states of consciousness beyond the testimony of consciousness, as if consciousness could be other than *conscious*. Lewes insists against experience that the conditions of the vital organs are known to us in consciousness, because they affect ganglia of the same general structure with those that are the media of mental activity. Thus, by a conception so adverse to experience that experience can give us no gleam of light in constructing it, he extends the facts of mind into the intellectually dark, unknown, organic regions below it, and so secures the data for a new series of explanations. These are explanations that explain nothing ; that mislead the mind by images impertinent to the phenomena under consideration ; that add new perplexities and leave old ones in full force. A consciousness which does not involve a knowing of *some kind*, an experience of a *definite order*, is so impossible a notion as to expound nothing, as to stand itself in most pressing need of exposition. How, then, is the state of his lungs or of his heart, at any given moment, known to one? As they would appear to the eye, or to touch; or as they would impress a physician; or as the causes operative in pains or in pleasures? The moment we undertake to give a definite empirical form to this assumed consciousness, we see that we have no such consciousness to receive it.

Murphy, sharing also this universal tendency to mingle mental and physical facts, regards intelligence, in his work on Habit and Intelligence, as "an attitude of all living beings, and co-extensive with life itself." * He proceeds, however, to say, "When I speak of intelligence, I mean not only the conscious intelligence of the mind, but also the organizing intelligence which adapts the eye to seeing, the ear for hearing, and every other part of an organism for its work. The usual belief is that the organizing intelligence and the mental intelligence are two distinct intelligences. I have stated the reason for my belief that they are not distinct, but are two separate manifestations of the same intelligence, which is co-extensive with life, though it is for the most part unconscious, and only becomes fully conscious in the brain of man." † We shall

* Vol. i., p. vi.   † Ibid.

more and more confound different things as we strive to deal with, and talk of unconscious intelligence. Nothing can be more remote from human experience than intelligence which is not intelligence, yet is set to do the work of intelligence. Whatever unconscious intelligence may be, when it is anything, it is something which we ought to sharply distinguish from intelligence proper, from conscious knowing. When such distinctions as these are blurred we can hope very little from the analytic process.

In a like confused and confusing way, Hamilton and a large number with him partially obliterate the dividing line between matter and mind, and blend their opposed phenomena, by insisting on sub-conscious states of mind, and offering them as potent factors in modifying and expounding consciousness. States of brain and conscious states, or states of mind, are both elements of the psychological problem equally certain, and perfectly distinct, each in its own order ; but beyond these two sets of phenomena we know of no others. We know of no phenomena which are not in the brain, nor yet in consciousness. We have no region in which to locate them. The figurative prefix *sub*, in sub-consciousness, does not help us, any more than would *sub*-space, or *super*-space. Neither have we any organs with which to reach the facts of such a region, nor yet any faculties with which to conceive them, or bring them forward as constituents of intelligible explanations. A *sub*-conscious state, where is it ? what is it ? what are its efficiencies ?

We can make no answer unless we are willing to regard it as a purely physical fact, a state of brain, and then trace, as we may be able, its connections with mental activity.

This brings us to an equivalent and much more plausible theory of blended phenomena, that of unconscious cerebration, so vigorously held by Carpenter, so vigorously urged by Ribot, so quietly assumed by almost all who unite psychology to science. The favorite phrase and the happy phrase is that of "unconscious cerebration." Few are aware how much a doctrine may be indebted to a fortunate phrase, and how misleading such phrases often are. They become citadels to which combatants retire after every encounter; talismanic catch-words which restore courage and strength after every overthrow. They hold on this way year after year, and once in vogue, have the appearance of a substantial presence that is rarely challenged. Let us challenge this new-comer before it is in possession of complete citizenship in the philosophical world.

Few, I think, have considered all that is involved in the phrase, "unconscious cerebration." The cerebral act as an unconscious cerebration, is called on to take its place with conscious acts of cerebration, to fill out the series, and maintain unbroken its intellectual connections. The fundamental fact, therefore, in a succession of mental states are the cerebrations. When these proceed in the right order, every end is reached, consciousness is an incident of the series which may or may not accompany it, and when absent, in whole or in part, does not affect its practical value.

It is plainly involved in this philosophy, then, that a certain cerebral activity is the exact equivalent of a certain mental state, is the very substance of that state, so much so that mental states can pass into other dependent mental states and so forward to conclusions, though unaccompanied by consciousness. Every phase of deliberation and volition, of imagination and feeling, and every varying combination of them, have an efficient cause in peculiar forms of nervous action. A thought about London thus involves an exact cerebral process which discriminates it from a thought about Liverpool or Paris or Pekin. Every possible object and every possible thought about, or feeling concerning, it, or volition toward it, implies an equally distinct cerebral state that occasions it. As there is no object in the universe which may not be the object of thought and a great variety of thoughts ; as very many of these may also be the subjects of feeling and action ; and as the possible combinations of these become wholly immeasurable, this doctrine of physical states that correlate with each one of them becomes very remarkable. A few ounces of matter called the brain, in its various transitions, transitions so distinct as to give instantly separable results in every man's experience, afford the equivalent of all that is or can be in the Universe. The brain is more than a microcosm, since it reflects not merely facts but every imaginary conception about them. We have reached by this philosophy neither simplicity nor comprehensibility. We do not say that such a multiplicity of distinct processes in the brain is impossible, but that the supposition is very extreme.

A still greater difficulty is, these succeeding acts of cerebration involve each other. Their dependencies are between themselves, and turn on physical conditions. The conscious products, those of thought, feeling, volition, are so secondary, that it is immaterial in any given case whether they disappear or are retained in the series. The conscious images will still come out on the canvas in an advanced stage of the process in due order and quality. In the diversion of children we sometimes so combine the hands that the light of a lamp will cast on the wall the image of a rabbit. The fingers imitate the play of the jaws in eating, and a sudden movement represents the spring of the animal. The mimic scene on the wall has but a remote resemblance, either in appearance or in fact, to the causes that occasion it. The lamp may be extinguished without arresting the motion of the hands. It may be relighted, and the pantomime is resumed at the point it has reached. We have a play of rabbits without any rabbits ; eating and leaping without either food, mouth or limbs ; and an apparently coherent series of actions with no direct connection whatever between them. Something of the same relation would, under this view of cerebration, lie between thought and thought, thought and feeling, and between all mental phenomena and their physical causes, the passing processes of the

brain. One thought seems to arise from another,
the first feeling to occasion the second, but this is
illusion. So does our rabbit appear to relish his
food, or in sudden fear to forsake it. For all that
there is no rabbit.

Under this view, pressed to its issue, the connections of thought disappear ; mental phenomena fall
apart; it is an accident of lights and screens,
whether they are present at all. The successive
transitions of unconscious cerebration have between
themselves no inherent reasons ; no connections
either of logic or imagination lie between them,
while the thoughts which accompany them are a
child's diversion on the wall, due to the molecular
play of the brain as the light of consciousness for
the moment streams through it. This again is the
subversion of mind, since thought is nothing of any
moment unless it, as thought, determines its own
connections, and settles its own convictions.
Thought cannot be suicidal in this way, and carry
back any value or rightfulness to its self-destructive
reasoning.

It will be well also to observe not merely the
extravagant conclusion involved in this doctrine,
but the exceedingly meagre supply of facts on
which it rests. Not one fact, really and fully pertinent to its proof, is forthcoming. We know
that there is a destruction of brain-tissue incident
to thought, hence we infer, naturally enough, though
the inference is quite in advance of the evidence,
that each given amount of mental activity is attended with an equivalent amount of cerebration,

and so with an equivalent decomposition of brain-tissue. We also know that states of brain are influential over states of mind. Out of these two facts we make haste to construct the theory of unconscious cerebration. Our primary facts are sunk out of sight under the immense burden of hypothesis imposed upon them. Because brain-tissue is destroyed by mental action does it follow that the accompanying cerebration occasions the thought, and has peculiarities exactly corresponding to its peculiarities? In the same way might it follow, that in lifting weights each motion of the muscles is specific and settles the character of the weight raised and its line of direction. The lifting of iron or stone or wood should imply diverse muscular states, and each movement up or down, east or west, its own equivalent muscular expression. The only efficient element in the destruction of muscle is the vigor of the effort. The form and direction of it are immaterial except as they bear upon its energy. Moreover, it is the form of the effort that determines the muscular state, not the muscular state that fixes the form. Is it not, then, more just to suppose that the same thing is true in the allied case of the brain, that the mind directs the effort, and that this effort tells on tissue by its vigor and not by its specific purposes. Till at least one case can be given in which a definite molecular state is shown to be the stated antecedent of an equally definite thought, this theory of unconscious cerebration has not made its first point in proof.

But it may be said, this step has been taken.

The hallucinations of disease, the misleading images
of insanity are directly traceable to states of brain
as efficient forces.   It would certainly be more in
order to adduce healthy than diseased conditions of
the nervous system in establishing the normal dependencies of the mind.   May not this be one
feature of a diseased condition, that the ordinary
control of the mind over its organs is lost, and the
healthy relation of activities reversed?   We should
not argue from the condition of a paralytic, or from
the spasms of tetanus, to the ordinary connection
of muscles and nerves.   One passing into insanity
is often only too conscious of the mastery which
new and dreadful impressions are gaining over him,
of the trepidation of the mind in their presence ;
and sometimes an energetic purpose may serve to
check or to overcome disease.   Waking from a
troubled dream, we are in the same way conscious
of our returning voluntary power, dispelling its
monstrous images, subduing its fear, and restoring
order and quiet to the thoughts.   It may easily be
that insanity is due to this very fact, that a diseased
state of the brain overpowers the mind, arrests its
control, and sends eddying back upon it conditions
of irritation and distortion it cannot order into clear
perception or correct thought.

But this proof of the philosophy, such as it is,
does not go far enough.   No specific state of the
brain, even in disease, has been shown to be the
condition of an equally specific hallucination.   Ha-
lucinations of a certain order are traced in a
general way to diseased tissue ; that is all.   No

exact mental product is thereby made referable to one exact molecular action. It may well enough remain true, so far as this proof is concerned, that the disease is a general disturbing cause; while the mental disorder incident to it is to be ascribed in its precise features to present and previous intellectual states. The abnormal action is not the mere shadow of the physical facts, but these introduce themselves as a disturbing agency into an experience with its own impulses and own laws.

This is the more probable as the mind is obviously affected by the state of bodily organs other than the cerebrum. The stomach, the muscles, the glands may control the imagery of dreams and modify the current of waking thoughts. Will the physicist now say, that to each state of digestion there are incident certain cerebrations, and to these fixed images? Such assertions as these assume the proof, they do not furnish it. They arise as deductions from the notion of an unbroken equivalence of forces passing inward from the physical to the mental world, while this is the very thing denied by the intuitionalist, the very thing to be proved by the physicist. To assume under a general physical axiom this equivalence, is to postulate furtively the truth of the conclusion, and then derive it from itself. The facts do not bear on their face this equivalence and transfer of causes. The common convictions of men do not accept it; and the initiatory proof of the doctrine is not furnished, till some precise thought is by necessary reference identified with some precise cerebration. Proof is

not to proceed under axioms applicable to purely
physical facts, since the fitness of the extension of
these axioms is the very point at issue.

If we grant this theory of unconscious cerebration it will bring with it no explanation, unless we
allow its advocates to set aside the inherent connections of thought, and resolve states of mind into
disjointed images, chasing each other over the field
of consciousness. The shadows of clouds on the
landscape are incidents of vapor, sunshine and
wind, and come and go under the operation of
forces not at all present in the apparent phenomena.
If we are willing to make this image the analogon
of mental processes, if we are willing to deny all
direct dependence of conclusions on premises, and
make them both the empty images of physical
things united only by a physical link, our theory
may seem to subserve some purpose. Yet it is immaterial whether it does or does not, for it has
proved that proof is a sequence of shadows, and one
sequence should be as logically significant as another. If it is not, if one series has not the value
of every other series, we must at once fall back on
that logical coherence of thought which we have just
now denied, or we cannot judge between them.
But if proof as proof disappears, what becomes of
our argument? If Hamlet is slain in the first
scene, where is our play in five acts?

If, however, by mere assertion we attempt
to maintain the integrity of the mental processes,
our unconscious cerebrations will still lose all power
of explanation. It is inexplicable how premises,

which lie below consciousness, can sustain conclusions in consciousness, how the mind can wittingly
take up a mental movement at an advanced stage,
having missed its primary steps. Unconscious
cerebrations as the equivalents of thought, as transitions to them and from them, are new perplexities, not the solution of old ones. How am I to
understand by virtue of what I have not understood ? Or, if I do understand, is not that the assertion of a *conscious* process co-extensive with comprehension ? Any other statement of the facts is
itself a riddle, not a solution. It is simpler to accept the first facts without exposition than to put
upon them these terms of explanation.

That we should remember at one time what we
cannot at another ; that we should be brighter in
the morning than in the previous evening ; that
fatigue should tell upon mental powers ; that fortunate thoughts should flash suddenly upon us ; that
creative moments should overtake the man of
genius, are facts not very perplexing till we add to
them this doctrine of unconscious cerebrations, a
steady moiling of the brain by day and by night
by which we make even time through the whole
term of our spiritual being. This *is* curious, a good
deal more curious than that the strong man sometimes shakes himself, and does a great work at once.
The labor of thought, under this theory of unconscious cerebrations, may be more and more disposed
of in hours of rest. Like the thrifty commercial
traveler, the man of letters may come forth refreshed from his palace-car at the last station, having

passed the night in sleep while the busy wheels of thought were revolving. Here is the long-sought royal road to knowledge.

That the mind like the body grows in power; that it is impaired by fatigue; that it puts forth on occasions sudden energies; that its activity is modified by physical conditions, these are ultimate truths in its constitution. Diligence also prepares the way for a discovery, a theory, an inventive mood, by returning often through protracted periods to the same topic, and so familiarizing the mind with all its features. The last result is thus the product of conscious activity, not unconscious cerebrations. This habit of thoughtfulness, productiveness, is a material difference between man and man.

The mind also has states of elevation, due partly to physical and partly to mental causes often too subtile for discovery, and these explain much hastily referred to unconscious cerebral labor.

New and great burdens immediately rest on this doctrine of unconscious cerebration. We are wont to be first impressed by the solutions which a theory offers, and only later to fully appreciate the additional difficulties which it brings with it. A peculiar state of brain is, by this hypothesis, made the efficient cause of each mental state or act. Our thoughts are given, retained and restored in direct dependence on physical forces. Not only is the brain thus made, as already pointed out, the seat of an infinite number of states, these states, in order that memory may be fully operative, must be so preserved as to be capable of easy repetition with-

out disturbance to each other or to new activity.
This susceptibility to fresh constructive movements,
this exact retention of old ones, must be held fast
amid all the decomposition and recomposition incident to activity and growth.   When the memory is
lost by disease this construction has fallen to pieces.
When it is restored by health these outlines of
thought have reappeared under the identical patterns.   All this is pure physical imagery of the
most improbable and inexplicable character, and
when it is all conceded, it fails to expound the facts
to which it is applied.   It remains in itself incomprehensible, extravagantly so, and tells us nothing
clearly about the mental states which accompany
it.   The only thing in these which it can be thought
to explain is their order of sequence, and this it explains by the utter subversion of that very intrinsic
dependence between our mental states which alone
interests us in them.

We shall, then, in oversight of all this accumulated rubbish of sub-conscious phenomena, of physical facts thrust in the place of mental ones,
proceed to discuss intelligence as intelligence, and
inquire into its origin and growth and grades
under its only known type, that of consciousness.
We start with the common convictions of men in
a belief in the integrity and relative independence of
the phenomena of consciousness, and we shall hope,
at the close of our inquiry, to possess additional
knowledge of the interaction of the two constructive elements of the world.   We have dwelt at
opening on the radical distinction between the two,

as it would be impossible for us to understand
comparative psychology, the slow evolution of the
intelligence now presented in man, without accepting the unique nature of the final product, the remoteness of the end from the beginning, the height
reached in our spiritual nature. It is the subtile and
prolonged interaction of two very distinct factors,
to wit, the physical and the intellectual ones, blend-
ing and combining in many ways without a loss on
the part of either of their distinctive natures, that
is to occupy us.

We are certainly right in the outset in accepting apparent facts as real facts, and holding apart
phenomena so distinct in form as those of matter
and mind, till an identity of nature shall be established between them. If we assume similarity
where it does not exist, we remove the very object
of inquiry. We must in the beginning accept an
apparent difference as a real difference, and wait for
investigation to establish, if it be established at all,
an agreement of forces under diverse manifestations.
It is to this inquiry, the slow superinduction of mental
upon physical facts, and the relation of the two as
indicated by this historic evolution, that we address
ourselves ; and no inquiry is more interesting, and
few more difficult. We can ill afford to prejudice
our success by too narrow forecast or too rigid
judgments. We must be content to see fully what
we see as the first condition of bringing to it any
comprehension. We must first recognize the grand
diversity of products in the midst of which we are,
before our synthesis of causes can be profoundly

instructive. If distances and differences disappear before us; if the deep waters always flow shallow under our keel, then our estimates will be trifling, our soundings superficial. We shall reach a vapid harmony of words by effacing the grand diversity of things ; we shall solve our problem by abolishing its conditions.

CHAPTER II.

PHYSICAL FORCES AS RELATED TO VITAL FORCES.

Two dangers accompany classification, or an effort to understand by resemblances the facts of the world in their relation to each other. The first is that of overlooking the gradations by which the points of extreme contrast are united, and so of regarding differences as more fundamental than they really are. This is the early error of immature knowledge.

The second danger is the reverse of this. When we discover the lines of demarcation to be vanishing ones, and that leading characteristics very slowly disappear as we approach and pass their boundaries, while other characteristics arise in the same gradual way as we leave these behind us, we jump to the opposite conclusion, and regard our distinctions of classes as relatively immaterial. The ultimate value of a difference depends on its real nature, and is not much modified by the steps by which it has been reached. The difference remains a fixed fact, a determinate feature in the final results, not reduced in its importance by intermediate gradations. These gradations instruct

36

us in the order of development, and help to define
the value of differences, but do not remove or essentially reduce the diversity which exists in the
results themselves, or destroy its worth as knowledge. Our knowledge is made rather the more
complete. Under a doctrine of development our
spaces in classification gain a double measurement,
that of sensible and constructive qualities, and
that of the length of the periods during which
these diversities have grown up. These two will
in large measure coincide, and serve to explain
each other. For illustration, the apparent difference between physical forces and mental activities
is the greatest possible, and the whole period of
development lies between these two poles. We do
not in classification stand simply on one peak, and
look across to another. We travel down a path of
descent to a line of union, and then thread our
way by one of ascent to the summit of its neigh-
bor. Now the predominance of pure physical
forces is separated from the prevalence of intellectual power by the whole diameter of being, equally
in the period occupied in its development as in the
apparent significance of the distinction; and so
we are doubly sure of our radical antithesis.

A fundamental difference as we have striven to
show between mental phenomena and physical
phenomena is that of consciousness, as the form-
element of the one, and that of space, as the form-
element of the other. Now it does not reduce the
value of this characteristic of the two sets of facts
that consciousness descends from one grade of ani-

mal life to a lower, and at length expires, like a
beam of light swallowed up in darkness, somewhere in the obscure regions of the inferior half
of this kingdom.   Mind remains none the less in
its complete form the realm of light and glory we
have all along thought it to be.   These measure-
less stretches of growth by which we approach the
luxuriant fields of intellectual activity ; first, the
blank, weary, never-ending desert ; then the single
dwarf shrub at long intervals ; then clustering
shrubs and new varieties ; then scantily clothed
fields ; and, at the very end of the journey, afflu-
ent life under a happy combination of higher conditions, are fitted rather to impress us with the
value of the diversities by which, in the intellectual world, a new element, that of consciousness, is
brought forward, fostered by nature, and deliber-
ately unfolded in complete spiritual power,

The processes that go on outside of consciousness are not, in their intellectual bearings, so very
unlike those that go on in it.   The difference lies
in the new, the inscrutable combining condition
which consciousness itself more and more distinctly furnishes, as its facts enlarge, and the significance of the powers it contains is felt.   The
molecular actions, the chemical and thermal forces
of a living body are not distinct from those operative in inorganic matter, yet none the less a highly
organized body, like that of man, does impress the
profoundest differences in final results on all the
processes that go on within it.   A knowledge of
physics and of inorganic chemistry in its closest

relations to organic chemistry does not disguise this profound diversity, but helps us to appreciate it rather. That thought is shallow indeed, that fancies, by any successes whatever in elementary facts, it shall master the secret of those agencies, so wonderfully combined and guided, which build up the human body, and treasure and transmit its tendencies. When we are discussing life, whatever we may choose to regard it, whether a force or a combination of forces, or a spiritual power, it is precisely these strangely new and most efficient conditions which it imposes on all that takes place within its circle that we need to consider, and these conditions lose none of their distinctions, none of their importance, because they have arisen slowly, now exist in many forms, and gather within the circuit of their activity the oldest agencies. This fact makes, however, a knowledge of the interactions which fall to purely physical and chemical forces preliminary to biology, while leaving the field of biology, in its rapid growth of differences, its new uses, and new combinations, as we pass from the margin inward, quite by itself.

Preliminary to a discussion of the facts of consciousness, we must know what are the primary forces on which it begins to be operative, when it first makes its appearance among them, and the way in which it slowly works them up into its now higher uses. But these primitive, physical facts we are now to regard in their intellectual rather than in their sensible features. This is our immediate purpose, to give in order the intellectual characteristics of strictly unconscious forces, those forces on which and with which the conscious powers and processes are to be built up when they arise. The simplest physical force is mechanical force, that force which expresses itself in the motion of masses. This motion of bodies of sensible magnitudes seems in all cases to arise out of forces that are primarily molecular. Gravitation is such a force; it lies between ultimate particles and there receives its first measurement and its final reference. Heat, a constant source of great movements, as in the atmosphere, or the ocean, or the earth's crust, or as in the steam-engine, is itself a molecular movement, and the product of molecular reconstruction. The same is true of animal strength. The source of it is muscular tissue, and the significant feature of this tissue is ready molecular change. Mechanical force, therefore, is only molecular force massed, and is constantly passing again into molecular movement. As a body is a combination of atoms, and may dissolve again into them, so the movement of masses is the harmonized movement of molecules, and may pass again into their disruptive movement. The significant intellectual feature of this fact is, that all mechanical force springs from inscrutable molecular forces, and that molecular forces, escaping all farther analysis, and known only in certain definite results, are the ultimate constituents of the world. The atoms of any substance express in reference to the atoms of other substances, certain forces or definite activities, and the molecules arising from these atoms in their various combinations in turn express new forces in reference to other molecules. Hence atomic forces become the seat and source of all forces, and of all mystery.   Atoms determine molecules, molecules settle properties, define physical and chemical activities, and the motion of masses.   Hence what we know as primitive, physical and chemical facts, the division of distinct elements into distinct atoms, the action of these atoms on each other in molecules, issuing in properties and motions, become the ultimate facts of the world, our first inscrutable, constructive terms. Any ultimate fact as incapable of farther analysis is a mystery, that is something given with no explanatory mode back of it.   Ultimate truths in mind, that is, axioms, are the plainest of all truths ; ultimate truths in matter, that is, atomic properties, are the obscurest of all truths.   The mind brings the clearest light to its primitive intuitions, and is more uncertain as to their application in experience ; it brings the least light to the first content of the senses.   This is material most alien to it, and its sense of knowledge increases only as it discovers the methods in which, under its own ideas, these inscrutable factors are combined. Here, again, its knowledge is one of relations, and not of ultimate facts.

What may be termed the rational characteristics of these primitive forces are, first, that their phenomena are referable, all of them, to some portion of space ; second, that they assume fixed forms under fixed conditions as ultimate facts in

the physical world ; third, that they all involve an
unphenomenal energy which admits of no farther
explanation ; and, fourth, that these energies, while
relatively fixed in form and permanent in being,
replace each other to some extent under a law of
equivalence in an inscrutable way. The first of
these characteristics is absolute. Every physical
discussion turns on facts that are located, on forces
that have points or lines of action. The second is
doubtless equally true, that causation is fixed in
the material world ; that its forces are permanent,
and hence its laws unchangeable. Yet this is a
fact of experience which we cannot fully verify
within its own field, and this field is narrowed by
the constant intervention of voluntary power. We
have, moreover, not only to accept ultimate qualities, like those of hydrogen, without explanation ;
but also that the same substance, as in the case of
oxygen, may assume two degrees of energy, or, as
in the case of carbon, may, in different forms, manifest very different sensible qualities ; and also that
compounds, as starch and cellulose, of the same
chemical elements and of the same molecular construction, are yet unlike in appearance and properties. If we refer in any case this change of qualities to a change in the arrangement of the atoms
within the molecule, we have simply added a new
dividing fact, but one which leaves the mystery of
method in each case precisely where it found it.
We have also, notwithstanding this permanence of
forces, to accept as an apparent fact the loss of
energy in the Universe by the dispersion of heat
and light.

The third characteristic, to wit, those ultimate energies to which we refer properties and motions, is a first term of knowledge given by the mind itself, and is that term by virtue of which the whole interplay of mind and matter is instituted, the whole framework of thought outlined. These molecular energies are the conditions of properties, and so of sensations. They thus give ingress to knowledge. They also offer themselves to the will as muscular strength, and so give egress to power. They are the first term both of knowledge and power, are the mediums by which mind, otherwise enclosed in the circle of its own consciousness, is put into communion with a substantial world exterior to itself. These unsearchable energies that meet the mind, and support it at every step, in thought and work alike, are the constructive terms which it carries with it everywhere.

The fourth characteristic, the limited substitution of these forces, one for another, in equivalent expressions, is a grand law of order and measurement among the phenomena of the Universe, yet this substitution is as inscrutable, and in its final principle as unphenominal, as the forces themselves. Chemical affinity, thermal energy, mechanical force, are translated into each other by no interior process within our knowledge.

Not only are molecules the seat of atomic forces expressed in physical properties, in chemical affinities, and in motion, there also arises in crystallization an orderly combination between them, which, while it acts on and by single molecūles, contemplates the general order of the product, and a variety of conditions removed from each other in space. The workman bears the brick to its own place in the building, but that place has been assigned it by a comprehensive plan. Even gravitation, acting in the single molecule, adjusts its energy to the number, amount of matter, and distance of all other molecules. Each simple substance that passes quietly from a free state, as that of solution, to one of solidity, has one or two crystalline forms which it assumes with the utmost exactness, as tested by the measurement of angles. As its purity is lost by the introduction of another element, the angles of its crystals are steadily modified. It is not easy to understand how the energies of crystallization can be purely molecular forces, since they seem to contemplate the entire crystal, and to be momentarily affected by its stages of structure in every part. The molecules are not merely laid in order, as bricks in a wall, but the form and dimensions of the whole work are operative each moment.

This is perhaps more obvious in the fact, that broken crystals may be repaired in a fresh solution ; and by the yet more observable fact, that if one of the angles of a crystal of alum be cut off, and the crystal placed in the solution resting on the face so made, a corresponding truncation, as the crystal grows, will appear on the opposite angle.*

It is difficult to refer facts of this character to

* Habit and Intelligence, vol. i. p. 75.

strictly molecular forces, able only to control the motions of single molecules, and not able to con-template the final product ; and equally difficult is it to find any other forces that can take into con-sideration the progress of the entire structure, and work toward a specified form of symmetry under specified conditions, and toward another under other conditions.

In the frost-work on the window-pane, or in the tree-like growth of crystals in solution, we have much freer and more complex arrangements, but arrangements so orderly and imitative that we can-not refer them to accident. Some of the forms of vegetable life are closely followed. A bed of cactuses grows up luxuriantly on a portion of the glass, they draw all the moisture to themselves, and leave the remainder of the pane clear. Arranging power is no more obvious in the plants themselves than in this mimicry of them. Under other con-ditions other forms of life are followed, but there is always a discernible tendency toward a particu-lar pattern, and an obvious consistency in follow-ing it out. Thus we have, before we reach life, regular mathematical figure, then the symmetry secured by the conformity of one angle of a crys-tal to the artificial conditions imposed on another angle, and finally a complex growth of forms hardly less free and beautiful than those of vegetable life itself. Vegetable and animal life, when they come, start with less complexity, less control of outline, less apparent relation than has already been reached in clustering crystals. The difference be-

tween the molecules of protoplasm and sarcode
and those of the crystalline solution is found in
the fact that the latter retain their freedom only in
a transition state through which they are passing
on to solidity, while the former remain indefinitely
active, and work in a more varied way toward more
remote and complicated ends. Yet in vegetable
life, and in large classes of animal life, the circulation slowly issues in a dead heart-wood or dead
coralline stem, or a dead shell, to which the constructive power is as much exterior as to the crystal. It is only in the higher animals that life remains in full possession of its material, and establishes itself in every part in permanent though by
no means in equal activity.

The first gain of what we regard as life over
crystalline activity is not, then, in form, but in a
freer and larger interplay of parts. Every portion
of the living globule of sarcode is sentient, and
active for the common end of growth. It extempo-
rizes at any point the needful organ ; moves toward,
lays hold of, absorbs and digests the required food.
Here, then, we reach those living forces which
in their variability, adaptability, and reciprocal relations to each other—relations which, if immediate in time, lie between objects more or less remote in space, and turn on no known physical energies—it is peculiarly difficult to regard as purely
molecular, since they are the means of controlling
the entire organism, and are at every stage modified by it, no matter what dimensions it may
reach.

In the plant, as in every living thing, we have two very different expressions of power : first, the molecular changes, the combinations and recombinations which take place under atomic forces in its several parts, changes allied to those we are familiar with in matter, and which have all along been ultimate with us ; and, second, that relation of members and functions, becoming ever more complex as we pass up, by which the plant or the animal is one organism, having one interest and one life. No molecular activities suffice to explain this order, since it is a combination of these activities outside of themselves, a government imposed upon them in reference to relations exterior to them, and momentarily changing with growth. No matter what molecular forces we may attribute to any or to all portions of the organism, the guiding power must constantly transcend their narrow sphere. They cannot be used to explain life, the relations of the whole to every part, the relations of each successive organism to those that have gone before it and those that are to follow it. Here is a series of immediate and remote dependencies that are habitually contemplated, that are in some way effective in each change, in each action and each organ each instant, and so are not referable to primitive or to fixed molecular forces. If we were to refer these variable and strangely extended energies to molecules, they must still be accepted as something quite new. The concentration of these organizing activities in gemmules, is an explanation neither physical, nor conceivable, nor empirical ; but one simply huddling the whole remainder of mystery in an unknown way into unknown things.

But something of this same power of definite arrangement has already been seen in the frost-work of a winter's morning. Something more remotely allied to it is also found in the growth of the world as a whole, in the nature of ultimate elements, their proportions, their union in development, and their slow evolution into the present order and beauty of the Universe. Ultimate molecular forces do not explain their fortunate conditions of interaction. We have not merely the definite nature of each element, but their relative amounts and the conditions in time and space which make of the combination a germ of order, the seed of the Cosmos. The ultimate molecular forces have thus a fitness for each other and their work, which we cannot overlook ; which, indeed, is the greatly significant thing, the moment we contemplate the Universe as a whole, the moment the reason puts its two great questions, questions equally just each in its own field—By what means ? and Why?

Here, then, from the beginning, and more manifestly as we progress, there are two ultimate terms, molecular forces and combining powers, the one as real as the other, the one as inscrutable as the other, as supersensible in final analysis. Though this combining power becomes more apparent as we move upward, it is present from the beginning, and institutes the first as certainly as the last movement in world-building. It may seem possible to say, that the molecular forces exclusively construct the physical world, yet the precision of their action, their variety, their proportions and relations to each other and their work, the most striking intellectual facts of all, are overlooked by this explanation. Some primitive forces may also be brought forward to explain the crystal and the crystal-plant, yet the varying symmetries by which they primarily appeal to the rational eye are again forgotten, or passed slightingly by. When we approach the plant and the animal, with a constant interplay of parts and transmission of structure, we are more than ever compelled to admit a constructive and controlling power, which in this domain the human mind has always recognized under the word, life. This combining power is a new, ultimate fact, is not a molecular force, but expresses itself in the way in which these forces are bent to wonderful uses. It is just as impossible, as intellectually impoverishing, to deny the second as the first of these two ultimate terms, the combining powers as the primary properties, the subtile oversight as the constructive force. If we force back the conception in one form it pushes itself forward in another ; if we reject life, its place is immediately occupied by "physiological units."

A stubborn effort has been made and is made to get rid of forces, and replace them with pure phenomena, with what success the student of philosophy knows. A more general effort, though one

theoretically less consistent, is made to escape presiding power, and substitute for it molecular force.
This labor, undertaken chiefly in the name of science, seems to us no more successful than the
former; the only significant intellectual facts, those
of relation, are wholly lost or greatly restricted
by it.

Incident to this effort is the idea of seeds or
germs as containing in themselves the typical
forces which are to be unfolded in the plant and
the animal. Take the cell or group of cells
through which in transmission the constructive,
hereditary tendencies of any portion of the human
race, in its specific qualities and individual variations, is passing. These cells are almost structure-
less, are in all sensible qualities the precise equivalents of a million other cells, ready in development
to move toward every quarter of the organic kingdom. With what incredible latent powers is such
a cell gifted, powers that have been accumulated
by the modifications of innumerable years, powers
a portion of which may show themselves suddenly
at the expiration of many more years! Therein is
gathered that central group of constructive tendencies by which the human body in its specific
type, with its great variety of members and its
complex functions, arising simultaneously and suc-
cessively, is to be built up; there are those rare,
national and family traits, and individual peculiarities, which are present mutually to modify each
other; there are those immediate and remote be-
nign or malign, normal or abnormal, inheritances,

which have found their way into the line of descent ;
there are the variations of sex, and of mental and
physical constitution as modified by sex, waiting
to be transmitted, as the case may be, through the
same or the opposite sex ; and there also are those
·recuperative and repairing powers that are to strike
in at any time, as disease or accident may give
them occasion. The river that in full volume
flows through the valley has not collected its
waters, drop by drop, from so many or so remote
places. Nor is this all ; by evolution we trace
back these cells to more primitive cells, and these
to others, till one cell may theoretically contain the
latent powers expressed in the entire organic
world. All the rivers of the globe are thus found
flowing through the eye of a needle. Yet, pressing the evolution one step farther back, this wonderful susceptibility condensed in the parent germ,
those innumerable realized tendencies expressed in
subsequent germs, all come forth from the inorganic nebulous mass, the seed of our present solar
system in its multiplicity of development, its rich-
ness of actual and potential life.

We must deny to this doctrine of germs, as
containing in themselves as latent forces the results that flow from them, any power of rational
explanation. Such germs are beyond all analogy,
as there is nothing in our experience which gives
any suggestion of their construction, or of any
such complexity of latent forces. The nearest approach to it is perhaps the number of mechanical
transmissions of force which can be impressed on

a large body of air or water ; but these forces are of one kind, and really afford neither the imagination nor the judgment any help. If we return to our cell, we are not merely utterly unable to understand how such an infinity of forces can possibly lie compressed within it, we are equally unable to understand how they came there, or being there can do the work assigned them. How can molecular forces, acting within their own narrow sphere, control a bulky organism, superintend its construction, and be cognizant of the passing conditions of its every part ? Do such primitive cells in multiplication impart their entire force to kindred cells ? or do they divide it with them ? If they divide and subdivide it, it must be quickly lost ; if they impart it entire, then new forces of the most wonderful kind are being momentarily created, or are being taken directly out of the environment of physical forces. Either the law of causation fails, since from one cell comes many equally endowed cells: or physical forces can yield directly any combination whatever of vital tendencies. If one cell or a few cells are the medium of this transfer, how do they control other cells or other molecules ? If all are the medium of the same powers, how does each fall into its own place, selecting from among its functions the one which is for the moment in order ? The notion of germs and seeds, as the transition points of all the patent and latent constructive powers of the vegetable and animal kingdoms, is, in whatever way we consider it, unintelligible, burdened with an amazing complexity of suppositions and inadequacy of results. The only fact that sustains it is, that certain causes are assigned to certain effects, but causes that are united to their effects by no known analogy.

This notion of germs as the medium of transmitted tendencies has been taken up with very little effort to make it clear, or to use it otherwise than as an obscure ultimate term taking a position that was left void to the thought by the denial of life. As an ultimate, unanalyzed factor, the chief question concerning it is, Which is the more rational reference of combining, harmonizing power, to matter or to mind, to a visible presence of forces which yet do visibly no part of the work that falls to them, or to an invisible power akin to its invisible functions? To the question so put, reason, it seems to us, has but one answer.

The facts of inheritance have given occasion to an effort to conceive more definitely this process of transmission. The most plausible and fully developed of the theories of heredity is that of pangenesis, presented by Darwin and enlarged by others. The substance of the theory is this: The fertilized ovum, which is the same in its characteristics in all Mammalia, and, though containing much of mere nutriment, is packed into a space not exceeding the size of the head of a pin, holds the separate gemmules which represent the controlling forces that are to build up all the different parts of the body, to rebuild them if need be, to induce in them at every stage of development in each generation and in successive generations every different phase of activity due to inheritance, and to receive and store up all tendencies that may be newly established.*

The specific organization of each animal and its individual characteristics are referred to gemmules, which hold their functions latent, or exercise and transmit them according to forces and affinities of their own. Thus we put back of one combination, the human body, another combination equally marvelous, that of gemmules in an ovum, and call this explanation, when our second term has no advantage over our first term except that of being infinitesimal. The tendency is identical with that by which we put forces as real being under phenomena, and then in the imagination strive to rehabilitate them as phenomena, and thus put a second layer of like facts under our first layer. So in science we play over and over again the old mythology. Everything is heaped on the back of a turtle, and the turtle left to shift for itself.

Such is the theory, and it is something every way wonderful. That must be a difficult subject to which it brings any relief. It is a theory purely theoretical ; it has in facts no starting points. We do not know of the existence of any such things as gemmules. Our ultimate chemical analysis of organic substances yields molecules and atoms of known properties, and our synthesis complex molecules, but neither discloses any gemmules or any

* Contemporary Review, Dec. 1875.

properties allied to those ascribed to them. In tracing the organic process itself we reach the ovum as its first term, but find in it no hint of farther organisms, of gemmules.

But this hypothesis not only rests on no known facts, it is startlingly complex, and becomes rapidly more so at each step. We are disposed to lay no great stress on the conceivable and the inconceivable — inconceivability may or may not constitute an objection — but certainly the extraordinary and the complex reflect, according to their degree, improbability on a theory, and in this theory they exist in the highest measure. Moreover, the growth of the theory is as surreptitious as its inception. New qualities and fresh conditions are added without stint to the gemmules, as a need for them is felt, and so the halting explanation is helped forward one stage more. Words are added to words, and when we have finished we have nothing but words on which to repose our faith. We have surrounded our facts by a scaffolding of purely *a priori* conceptions.

Nor can the theory, with all its constructive license, give plausibility to its conclusions. It is not at all plain how these gemmules, if we grant them to exist in incredible numbers and with an exhaustless variety of tendencies, can do their work. Let us make the supposition that we have a brick building to construct, to be made of many thousand bricks, and bricks of very many patterns. We have sample bricks of each of these kinds as our constructive material. With what properties must we endow them in order that they may go forward with the construction? First, they must be able to multiply themselves indefinitely; secondly, they must be able to put themselves in the right place, and bring forward their various forms at the right instant; thirdly, in order to accomplish this, they must in some way have an oversight of the entire structure, and so comprehend its every stage and every exigency.

Now no mere atomic forces, acting blindly from local centres, can do any such work. Our bricks must be made intelligent, for they have before them that elaborate combination of parts which is the distinctive work of intelligence. But our supposition is incomparably less complex than that involved in the construction of the human race, man by man, through the agency of gemmules. Here no two parts are identical in structure, functions and relations, while these relations shift at each transfer in slight ways and decisive ways, in obscure ways and subtile ways, and are by the whole movement resolved into a perpetual flux, whose immediate and remote terms momentarily affect each other in lines of causation quite too deep for physics.

When, therefore, the theory of pangenesis talks about affinities among gemmules as a means of explaining the movements, the moments and the proportions of activities, the relations of parts and parts, functions and functions, growths and growths to each other in a race like that of man, it is simply surrounding atoms with a halo of light, with intelligent powers, in order that matter in molecules, in a way wholly alien to our experience of it in masses, may do the work of mind. We retreat with our suppositions into infinitesimals, and so escape contradiction. In this region we know nothing and may assume everything. Properties of which we find no trace in the aggregate we fearlessly assign to the atom.

The powers we do assign are not in their nature atomic, they are those of supervision, those of intelligence. Which, then, is the simpler supposition, the one most accordant with experience in its own range, that thought, pervasive, spiritual power does this work of thought? or that matter, when it sinks below the range of the senses, is endowed with tendencies purely intellectual in their functions? By such a supposition we sponge out the first dividing lines of knowledge; mind and matter flow into each other; we belittle our constructive thought, and destroy its work thus far.

The conception, on the other hand, of a spiritual presence which uses and combines the atomic forces of the world is in strict harmony with our experience. Our own minds, without appearing among the physical forces of the body as a part of them, do in some inscrutable way control them for their own ends, and make them minister to a rational life. As our spirits are the inspiration of our bodies, so may "the lives," the Supreme Spiritual Power in its divided yet concurrent action, be the inspiration and overshadowing power of the physical world. We, at least, must reject germs as either the mediate or ultimate fountains of the wisdom of the world. The streams of thought do not for us deepen into perennial springs as we press inward toward the secret recesses of physical forces. These mountains, high and grand as they are, yield nothing but dust save as they are rained on by the heavens above them. Life is not force, it is combining power ; it is not local, it is pervasive ; it is not the emanation of matter, but the product and presence of mind.

If agreement with experience is any test of a theory, then the supposition of an intelligent power in the world has a decisive advantage over any theory of *quasi* intelligent matter. By the supposition of a Supreme Spiritual Presence we transcend our experience at one point only. We assume that the Divine Mind can work in matter without the intervention of a nervous system, that spiritual power can be distributed without these conditions of distribution peculiar to us. It is a favorite accusation of the scientist against theology, that it is intolerably anthropomorphic in its methods. Is not the scientist intolerably anthropomorphic in his methods, when he will not believe in a Spiritual Presence in the world because there are no visible cerebrum, cerebellum and medulla oblongata ? Simplicity and experience are with those who leave with matter its fixed, atomic forces, and with mind its combining, supervisory power ; who distinguish substance and form, material and purpose, matter and mind, and put them as first terms of thought in eternal interplay.

It is incident to our lives as finite that their powers should be conditioned, and these conditions rest back on this point, a nervous system, whose resources are quickly exhausted. Moreover, matter is necessarily to us, as dependent beings, wholly foreign ; its activities are another's activities. In neither of these respects is the Supreme Intelligence in our image ; and while we securely reason from agreements to agreements, from intelligence to intelligence, we justly allow to enter those differences of relation to the Universe about us which must so plainly lie between the finite and the Infinite. The absence of all analogy snaps the threads of thought. So is it everywhere. The literalist and the supersensualist can neither prosper. If we make ourselves the slaves of experience, our reasoning will either be servile or fugitive ; it can never be bold, sound and free ; it can never be broadly rational.

We start, then, our cosmic, constructive processes with two elements, forces whose first manifestation is in space, and which testify to their own external and permanent being by their transient phenomena in consciousness ; and powers which control and combine these forces ; powers which are addressed to the intellect by instituting those relations which are the hidden meaning, the true significance, of the language of phenomena. Neither of these offer themselves as intelligence, but are the products of an Intelligence that abides back of and above them both.

The Supreme Intelligence accepts at once in

its products the laws and conditions of reason, both because it itself is rational, and because it addresses itself to that coming intelligence which is the fulness of the creative process.   Hence forces as fixed material take on themselves a variety of laws, that is, they submit themselves as fixed premises to the coherent ends and uses of the reason that called them forth.   The living, plastic powers also, though moving toward variable and enlarging ends, accept the limiting conditions of reason which press in upon them, as, resting backward, they stand in the relation of results to previous circumstances, or, pushing forward, they become means to farther ends.

Both forces and powers are ultimately referable to a Supreme Intelligence, and, moving onward in evolution, make conquests and give conditions for those grades of finite intelligence which constitute the kingdom of conscious life.   We need, then, in rising step by step, till we have mounted the stylobate on which our spiritual temple rests, to see how these foundations of intelligence have been laid, what are its conditions, what has been given us by anticipation in forces and what in powers, that we may afterward see with what resources the first germs of conscious life are occupied, and how, from stage to stage and mastery to mastery, it climbs up to its present position in man, while still reaching down in direct influence to the primitive, physical facts of the world.   We now, in our discussion, pass on to life ; and though we have as yet caught no light of consciousness, no single

spark of intelligence struck out of the flinty material about us, we have, in the material itself, the
rapidly accumulating conditions of an associative
and a rational experience, when consciousness and
reason shall at length offer themselves.

Every step of development, without containing
the next step, contains the conditions which prepare the way for it. The whole thus becomes a
growth, whose internal forces are watched over and
nourished by a spiritual environment.

CHAPTER III.

VEGETABLE LIFE.

It is not necessary for us to discuss farther the nature of life. Whatever that nature may be, whether life is simply a vague word by which we indicate certain complicated combinations of physical forces, set up in their strange equilibrations by an activity of their own ; or whether we regard it as an inborn presence, a plastic power by which such combinations are secured, maintained and carried forward, it stands, in either case, for certain facts, the same to all ; for processes which have a scope and harmony and laws of their own. It is not our purpose to give anything like a complete statement of the functions covered, in the vegetable kingdom, by the word life, but only to direct attention to some of those salient features which will serve to impress upon us afresh the number, variety and subtile character of those powers that we carry up with us in passing from vegetable to animal life. Kindred activities we may suppose to have a kindred source in both kingdoms. Any explanations we may later bring to the faculties of animals should be in harmony with what we meet with lower down ; should fully embrace the large initial terms which we bring with us in coming up to the higher realm from the region of purely vegetative activity. Processes, the counterparts of those we find in plants, do not in animals call for any new reference ; nor demand for their solution a conscious, intellectual existence. Whatever is to be ascribed to intelligence must, as a whole, lie beyond that already referred to vegetative life.

The chemical laboratory of the entire organic world is the green tissue of plants, more especially their leaves. Here inorganic material is turned into organic material, the food of plants and animals, and this with a large consumption of force. The process is one of extended deoxidation, and hence one which takes up and stores in the product all the energy which may afterward be given out in its reoxidation, either as food or as fuel. This chemical activity of the leaf, which is immense in itself, and of most immediate interest to all living things, is that termed by Sachs assimilation.* By it inorganic material is transformed into high organic compounds, holding in their mobile structure a large reserve of force, enabling them afterward to pass by easy metamorphosis into other vegetable and animal products. They thus become the material of every constructive, organic process in plants and in animals. In metamorphosis they yield new material, in degradation new force. Thus the first and by far the greatest or-

* Text-book of Botany, p. 626.

ganizing labor, as regards the energies employed, goes forward in the leaf. It is that by which the material for all the various forms of growth is furnished, material already of so facile a character, the storehouse of such forces, that it can in one or other of its forms pass into all the compounds of the plant and animal, itself furnishing in the transition the energy expended. 'The reserve materials stored up in different seeds, tubers, bulbs, the starch, the various kinds of sugar, inuline and oil, are of the same physiological value, inasmuch as these substances can replace each other in the formation of new organs, and also furnish the supply for a variety of substances found during growth, such as vegetable acids, tannin, coloring matter.'* The *formative materials* of the plant and so of the animal, starch, sugar, inuline, the fats, the albuminoids, receive their constructive character in the leaf, they then pass freely into other organic products, partially replacing each other in the process. This constant transfer between organic compounds is termed by Sachs metastasis. It is secondary to assimilation, which with him means the raising of inorganic to organic material.

Assimilation, the primitive member of the entire process, takes place exclusively in the green tissue of the plant. Its two conditions are chlorophyl and sunlight. The plant alone—we are not, however, speaking of any partial action of the lowest forms of animal life—yields these delicate conditions under which sunlight employs its immense

* Text-book of Botany, p. 629.

energy, and rapidly furnishes the material of all growth. We are simply to observe the delicacy, the energy, the inscrutability, the self-perpetuating character of this vegetable activity by which all the organic activities of the world are maintained. Without chlorophyl there is no growth; the sunlight, that noiseless cataract of force, descends in vain; there are no conditions for receiving and storing its energy. Yet chlorophyl is itself the product of this very process, a process, therefore, which infolds its own conditions, and is reciprocally interdependent in every portion of it. The relation of the seed to the plant and of the plant to the seed, each begetting and each begotten, is thus a typical fact. We have at once a self-sufficient circular movement, whose point of production we cannot indicate. This simple orbit of revolution found everywhere in the vegetable kingdom, with the ten thousand distinct forms it assumes and steadily maintains; this institution in every vegetable product of so difficult and wonderful and wonderfully varied a process, is our first term in organic life. We have from the outset a complex balance of functions sustaining themselves by motion, by perpetual interchange.

But not only does the plant offer in the leaf these exceptional conditions under which sunlight can build up organic compounds, in a way so free, and in amounts so large, it maintains these conditions as incident in each case to a complete system of growth, and one which involves a constant metastatis of formative material into a great variety

5

of permanent products which together constitute
the plant. Though the physical energy expended
in this metamorphosis may be furnished by the
compounds themselves, the conditions under which
it takes place in their great complexity, and the
ends to which it is made subservient in their great
variety, are maintained in each plant by its own
specific, organic power. The peculiar thing in
each is, the relation to each other and to the whole
of these transformations; and this organizing
movement, though narrow, is in itself as complete
in the vegetable as it is in the animal. This precise combination of precise functions in a specific
living thing expresses at once a thoroughly organic
power, and receives enlargement, not displacement
in the animal kingdom. The confining of organic
processes in the animal to metastasis, the dropping
away of the contrasted power of assimilation, in
some respects the greater of the two, is but one
of many illustrations of the intimate way in which
the higher development is built out of and on the
lower one, and of the manner in which a higher
movement modifies a lower and avails itself of it,
while reserving its own functions in an untrammeled
way to itself. The freedom in motion and in the
conditions of growth in the animal kingdom is
due largely to the fact that the immediate material
of growth is furnished to it, not manufactured by
it. The animal prospers where the plant would
perish, as it is comparatively independent of light
and external heat.

Incident to the growth of the plant is the constant transfer of constructive material, is circulation. The water and the crude ingredients of the sap are taken in at the root. This sap is trans-ferred to the leaf, or other green tissue of the plant, and there by assimilation laden with con-structive material. So enriched it is ultimately taken to the surfaces of growth, in exogenous plants to the cambium layer. If this circuit were a direct one, distinct fluids passing by distinct channels to their destination, it would still be inex-plicable. But it is very far from being a simple circulation. If we take a single tree, as a maple, to guide our conceptions, we shall see that the points of ingress through the roots are many and widely scattered, the leaves to which the sap is transferred are alike numerous and broadly distrib-uted, while the cambium layer, where the work of construction goes on, envelops the entire tree. In this circulation there is only a partial specializa-tion of office, the same cells are the channels of movement in various directions, and for various material.

"There is a peculiar motion of circulation of the fluid contents of every living cell called cyclo-sis or rotation of sap, and there is a general move-ment of fluids upward and downward in the entire plant which may be named circulation of sap." *
This irregular transfer of sap largely through the same cells between these irregular series of points or surfaces for constructive purposes would be curious enough and inexplicable enough, even if it

* Prof. Henfrey, Agriculture of Mass., 73-4, p. 177.

were constant and expressed all the facts. But it is not constant. Very much constructive material is reserved in the sap and elsewhere for long periods, and, when the exigency of use arises, is brought rapidly forward. There is thus within the larger circuit, or incidental to it, a great deal of circulation which does not contemplate an immediate want of the plant, which is not driven forward by the changes incident to a constructive process actually going forward. Sap is returned to the root, and is reserved in various parts of the tree, and produced at once on occasion. Thus this affair of transfers in the plant becomes exceedingly complex, and when we contemplate it as leading to well-ordered and uniform results in each species, exceedingly wonderful. Moreover, these results are by no means the same in different species. The oak puts forth tremendous energies when it wakes up in growth, and in a few days outlines and largely completes the work of the season. Other trees, like the willow, toil slowly, and devote the whole season to growth. The maple has times when the sap is at flood and goes streaming through its channels, and also times of inaction when its sluggish currents scarcely creep on their way. This activity is not provoked by any growth of the buds, but helps itself to determine their growth.   .

The forces that are relied on to explain this immense and spasmodic work of circulation are not sufficient for their purpose. This point is distinctly put and vigorously supported in the paper by Pres. Clarke, already referred to in the Agricultural Reports of Massachusetts. Yet the opposite statement is generally made, and by high authorities. Says Sachs: "This much appears certain that the ultimate forces concerned are always capillarity and diffusion—in the broadest sense of the term " *

But these two forces signally fail to account for the well-ordered issue of the circulation, for the way in which it adapts itself both to the immediate and the remote wants of the plant, for its fitful, irregular movement in the same plant, for its specific types of movement in different plants. We believe that they also fail to sufficiently explain the fact of a single hour in the circulation of a single tree, as a rock maple or a black birch, looked at simply as a process of mechanical transfer. We must recognize, therefore, first, an organic, plastic power of some sort, no matter what we call it, expressed by the order of the whole movement in its complicated interplay toward a single end, the growth of the plant. And we must also seek, secondly, for more elementary forces than these two of capillary attraction and diffusion, in order to furnish the energies directly active in circulation. The first of these needs, that for permanent organic power, all the facts, looked at in any wise, collective way, emphasize ; the second, that for elementary forces, other than the two mentioned, is supported by various considerations, by the ease with which a sucker in a root will change the cir-

* Text-book of Botany, p. 601.

culation, and draw its nourishment either upward
from the portion below it, or downward from the
parts above it; by the surprising force with which
the sap is at times driven upward in the tree, and
yet the almost immediate cessation or reversal
even of this power; by the fact that a root wholly
severed from the parent stem will impel the sap
outward at the section with great energy, though
there is no such loss of sap at the extremities of
the roots by a circulation in the opposite direction;
and by the extraordinary difference between trees
similarly situated, in the times of the flow of sap,
in the amount of the flow, and in bleeding at
wounds. These and like facts show a variety and
discrimination in results hardly to be attributed to
such general and uniform forces as capillarity and
diffusion. We will give a very few of the many
experiments of Pres. Clarke to illustrate the vigor
and decision of movement in the circulation of
sap.

"A gauge was attached to a sugar-maple
March 31st. The mercury was subject to constant and singular oscillations, standing usually in
the morning below zero, so that there was indicated a powerful suction into the tree, and rising
rapidly with the sun until the force indicated was
sufficient to sustain a column of water many feet
high. Thus, at 6 A. M. April 21st, there was a suction into the tree sufficient to raise a column of
water 25.95 feet. As soon as the morning sun
shone upon the tree the mercury suddenly began
to rise, so that at 8.15 A. M. the pressure outward

was enough to sustain a column of water 18.47 feet in height, a change represented by more than 44 feet of water. On the morning of April 22d the change was still greater, requiring for its representation 47.42 feet of water. These extraordinary fluctuations were not attended by any peculiar state of the weather, and happened twelve days before there were any indications of growth to be detected in the buds." * " On the 20th of April two gauges were attached to a large black birch, one at the ground and the other thirty feet higher. The next morning at 6 o'clock the lower gauge indicated the astonishing pressure of 56.65 feet of water, and the upper one of 26.74 feet. The difference between the indications of the two gauges was thus 29.92 feet, while the actual distance between them was 30.20 feet, so that they corresponded almost precisely as if connected by a tube. In order to learn if the same principle would prevail, if the upper gauge was moved, it was raised twelve feet higher. The same correspondence continued through nearly all the observations of the season, notwithstanding the gauges were separated by 42.20 feet of close-grained birch-wood." † These facts, as presented by Pres. Clarke, would seem to indicate that the sap above the gauges was not sustained either by attraction or diffusion, but rested on the sap below as a dead weight. The following experiment traces the force of injection still deeper into the root : " A root was followed from the trunk to the distance of ten

* Agriculture of Mass., 73–74, p. 187.   † Ibid. p. 188.

feet, where it was carefully cut off one foot below
the surface, and a piece removed from between the
cut and the tree. The end of the root thus entirely detached from the tree, and lying in an hori-
zontal position at the depth of one foot in the cold,
damp earth, unreached by the sunshine, and for
the most part unaffected by the temperature of the
atmosphere, measured about one inch in diameter.
To this was carefully adjusted a mercurial gauge,
April 26th. The pressure at once became evident,
and rose constantly, with very slight fluctuations,
until at noon on the 30th of April it had attained
the unequalled height of 85.80 feet of water. This
wonderful result showed that the absorbing power
of living birch rootlets, without the aid of any of
the numerous helps imposed upon them by ingenious philosophers, such as osmose, exhalation, dila-
tation, contraction, oscillation, capillarity, etc., etc.,
was quite sufficient to account for the most essential of the curious phenomena connected with the
circulation of the sap." *

All the use we wish to make of these statements is to show that there is in some way present
in the plant a power of wonderful energy, as indicated by its mastery of forces, and of great wisdom, as shown by the constructive service to
which it puts them. If the forces involved in this
growth are all gathered up from the physical and
chemical activities that lie below, as they probably
are, yet the uses made of them, their changeful
activity and sudden repression, their combination

* Agriculture of Mass., 73-74, p. 189.

into the habit of each species, a habit thoroughly subservient to its own methods of growth, still remain the chief factor in the organic process. To this intellectual element, we shall be justified, as we go higher, in referring all like constructive action. This we single out and bear with us as an inscrutable, plastic power, offering explanation to all kindred organic results.

We wish to enforce this result a little more before we leave it, and to observe some of the more surprising directions in which vegetable life, as contrasted with sensitive animal life, is extended. This constructive power involves, aside from its general organizing functions, many peculiar adaptations which, in their singular fitness and immediate dependence on external conditions, carry us very far on toward the increased sensitiveness and specialized activities of the animal kingdom. Thus a tendril, as soon as it has clasped a support, commencing at a point intermediate between its extremities, forms, by a twisting movement round itself, a double coil running toward each end. It thereby slowly tightens the bond which holds the climber, and makes it elastic. A tree, like the oak, in the deposit of the material of growth, fortifies a heavy branch, leaving the centre or pith quite in the upper half, bracing the limb strongly and gracefully below as it passes into the trunk, and interlacing the fibres of the two in the strongest way. The round bowl of the elm, with like fitness, raises sharp butments with deep interspaces, as it passes by its heavy roots into the soil.

A poplar, growing in the track of the wind, will convert the circular section of its trunk into an elliptical one, with its largest axis in the direction of the current.

We do not need to dwell on these special adaptations as they are not after all so much to our purpose as that habitual control of the entire organic movement which incidentally takes on these and a thousand other passing phases.

A second consideration in vegetable life is the immediate discrimination it involves. If discrimination were the proper test of consciousness here would be consciousness. The radicle and the plumule part company, the one working its way into the soil and darkness, the other searching for air and light. Totally diverse tendencies possess them from the outset, and they at once accommodate themselves to all the conditions for carrying them out. The problem of positions and relations is solved in the most direct way. The seed germinates on the decaying stump, and the roots descend along the sides into the soil beneath. In the same discriminating way the buds push upward, or to the right, or to the left, in search of the strongest light. The roots also find out the places of moisture and nutriment, and spread in those directions. Growth is not equal in all open spaces, but within limits selects the lines of development, and accommodates itself to circumstances. In many other ways is this recognition of relations and variation of growth in obedience to them observable.

If the leader of the balsam or spruce is broken, it supplies the place with a lateral. If a tree has attained undue height in the shade, when this shade is removed it sends out lower branches to strengthen the trunk. I once planted twenty-five European lindens which had been grown in a nursery and reached considerable height with very little strength. For several years they made no upward growth, but put forth sprouts freely up and down the stem. If these were stripped away, they were replaced, and the trees did not resume their normal growth till the bodies had been trebled in size. They thus fitted their development exactly to their new conditions, with an adaptation of means to ends as unmistakable as that indicated by cutting them back at the time of planting. Pines in the forest trim themselves rapidly, dropping their lower branches and sending up higher and higher those smooth, majestic trunks in which are found their chief beauty and value. This habit is incident to the absence of light, but seems something more after all than its direct effect, as the young pine will still grow at the base of trees that are losing freely their lower branches.

The vine, whose leaves have been disheveled in removal or in training, begins at once to readjust itself to the light, to accept and adopt new circumstances. Flowers, in their modes of presentation, in their times of opening, in their movements, put themselves actively in adjustment with the sunlight, sometimes in acceptance, sometimes in rejection, sometimes in gradation. Climbing

plants of Central America are said to show decided likes and dislikes in the trees they twine
about, refusing some altogether.*

The most striking examples in plants of discrimination of external conditions and direct response to them, are those so fully presented by
Mr. Darwin, in his volumes on Insectivorous Plants
and Climbing Plants. A few of the facts given by
him will subserve our purpose. The first brought
forward are found in his work on Insectivorous
Plants. Many plants, belonging to very different
species, respond by movement to irritation, and
are thus enabled to catch and feed upon insects.
In the common sun-dew, glands located in the centre of the leaf, when excited by contact, transmit
an impulse to marginal tentacles, and these slowly
gather in towards the centre, and freely close over
it. The time occupied by the movement depends
on the size of the object, on the soluble matter of
the proper kind it contains, on the vigor of the
leaf, on its previous contraction, and on temperature.

A living insect acts more efficiently than a
dead one, and one with thin than one with thick
integuments.† Thus the plant at once responds
to a half-dozen different conditions, meeting each
with its own measure of motion. But not only
does movement follow close on the appropriate
irritation, the glands involved pour forth an increased amount of fluid, and this not simply when

* Popular Science Monthly, vol. iii. p. 81.
† Insectivorous Plants, p. 9.

in contact with the insect, but as they approach it on all sides. The secretion also changes its nature and becomes acid.* A true digestive process, both in its mechanical and chemical elements, is thus established at once in the leaf of a plant by the presence of a digestible object, as much so as in the stomach of an animal. This is done, not merely in advance of that intelligence ordinarily developed in the capture of food, but also in advance of its usual instrument, a nervous system. If the insect alights on the margin of the disc, it is entangled by the secretion, rolled inward to the centre of the leaf by the contraction, and there digested by the aid of fluids, closely allied to gastric juices.† Thus a power which only recently has been proved to belong to the animal kingdom, the direct modification of the secretion of glands by irritation, is also included in organic vegetable life.

The discrimination of the plant is often of the most delicate character. The nitrogenous nature of the irritant is of great moment, and it must "literally rest on the glands." The pressure of a particle weighing only the $\frac{1}{78740}$ of a grain is sufficient to occasion movement, though "it is extremely doubtful whether any nerve in the human body, even in an inflamed condition, would be in any degree affected by such a particle supported in a dense fluid."‡ There is also not merely this original delicacy of touch, but a variation of it to suit special cases. "When the motor impulse

* Insectivorous Plants, p. 14.   † Ibid. p. 16.   ‡ Ibid. p. 33.

comes from one side of the disc, the surrounding tentacles, including the short ones in the middle of the disc, all bend with precision toward the point of excitement, wherever this may be situated. This is in every way a remarkable phenomenon; for the leaf falsely appears as if endowed with the senses of an animal." *

In the Dionæa, " the sensitiveness of the filaments is of a specialized nature, being related to a momentary touch rather than to prolonged pressure; and the touch must not be from fluids, such as air or water, but from some solid object."† The close alliance of this discrimination of the plant to true touch, is seen in the fact that it responds to momentary more readily than to prolonged contact; and its affiliation in form to intelligence in the fact that it distinguishes against water and air, as the sensitiveness of its structure would otherwise be wasted on rains and winds.

In the Venus' fly-trap the irritation occasions a much more rapid movement. The animal is captured by the quickness with which the leaf closes, and the glands take part by their secretion in the digestion only of the insect, not in its retention. In this plant the spikes which bristle on the margin of the leaf interlock with each other in closing, so as to allow the escape of very small insects, and to retain those only which promise a reasonable return to the plant for its labor. The leaf declines to waste time on the bug if he is not big enough to pay for the candle.

---

* Insectivorous Plants, p. 276.   † Ibid. p. 292.

In the somewhat large and varied class of insectivorous plants, we find many ways of responding slowly and rapidly, in physical movements and organic secretions, to influences of wonderful delicacy, both as to amount and character. The sensibilities of a nervous system are more varied, but are hardly more striking in special cases. We are to credit then to vegetable life the power to discern exceedingly slight external stimuli, and to respond to them in a variety of functions through an extended organism.

Climbing plants present a similar wonderful susceptibility to outward conditions. They also in new directions anticipate a sensitiveness belonging to the nervous structure of animals. Mr. Darw.n is again the chief authority. The remarkable features in the conduct of these plants are the slow revolution, in a larger or smaller circle, of the upper extremities, in search of a support; the manner in which a support is closely wrapped when it has been found; in some cases, the revolution of the leaves of the plant, with a like grasping power in the petioles; in still other instances, a similar motion of tendrils, and an extreme sensitiveness to all the conditions connected with a full discharge of their office.

The first of these peculiarities, the revolution of the free extremity of the climbing plant, is the most simple, and implies no adaptation to the immediate circumstances. As soon as an object is touched, the same revolving movement assumes the the form of pressure, and slowly winds the plant,

if the character of the support admits of this result, tightly about it in the direction of revolution.
That the climbing plant should take on a motion
so peculiar to its method of growth; that this
motion should be confined to the extremity of the
plant for a limited period, and that it should be displaced in part by the pressure of clasping leaves
and tendrils, all show an organic mastery of external conditions approaching that which we find in a
more complete form in higher life. The sensitiveness in some instances of the petioles, and more
frequently of the tendrils, of climbing plants, is a
much more remarkable forecast of later organic
functions. On this point we quote freely from
Darwin. The first passage bears on the sensitiveness of clasping petioles to contact, the second on
the sensitiveness of the tendrils of the Bignonia
to light, and on their general conduct. "The
petioles are sensitive to a touch and to excessively
slight continued pressure, even from a loop of soft
thread weighing only the one-sixteenth of a grain ;
and there is reason to believe that the rather thick
and stiff petioles of Clematis flammula are sensitive
to even much less weight if spread over a wide
surface. The petioles always bend toward the side
that is pressed or touched, at different rates in
different species, sometimes within a few minutes,
but generally after a much longer period. After
temporary contact with any object, the petiole continues to bend for a considerable time; afterwards
it slowly becomes straight again, and can then react. A petiole excited by an extremely slight

weight sometimes bends a little, and then becomes accustomed to the stimulus, and either bends no more or becomes straight again, the weight still remaining suspended. Petioles which have clasped an object for some little time can not recover their original position. After remaining clasped for two or three days, they generally increase much in thickness, either throughout their whole diameter or on one side alone ; they subsequently become stronger and more woody, sometimes to a wonderful degree ; and sometimes they acquire an internal structure like that of the stem or axis."* "On another plant three pairs of tendrils were produced at the same time by three shoots, and all happened to be differently directed. I placed the pot in a box open only on one side, and obliquely facing the light ; in two days all six tendrils pointed with unerring truth to the darkest corner of the box, though to do this each had to bend in a different manner. Six turret-vanes could not have more truly shown the direction of the wind than did these branched tendrils the course of the streams of light which entered the box."† "When a tendril has not succeeded in clasping a support, either through its own revolving movement or that of the shoot, or by turning toward any object that intercepts the light, it bends vertically downwards, and then toward its own stem, which it seizes, together with the supporting stick, if there be one. A little aid is thus given in keeping the stem secure. If the tendril seizes nothing, it soon withers away and

* Climbing Plants, p. 81   † Ibid. p. 98.

drops off."* "Knowing that the tendrils avoided the light, I gave them a glass tube blackened within, and a well-blackened zinc plate; but they soon recoiled from these objects with what I can only call disgust, and straightened themselves."† "I have watched a tendril, half of which had bent itself at right angles round the sharp corner of a square post, bring every single hook into contact with both rectangular surfaces. The appearance suggested the belief that though the whole tendril is not sensitive to the light, yet that the tips are so, and that they turn and twist themselves toward any dark surface. Ultimately the branches arrange themselves very neatly to all the irregularities of the most rugged bark, so that they resemble in their irregular course a river with its branches, as engraved on a map."‡ The following passages summarize the action of tendrils: "With most tendril-bearers the summit of the stem or shoot projects above the point from which the tendril arises; and it is generally bent to one side, so as to be out of the way of the revolutions swept by the tendril. In those plants in which the terminal shoot is not sufficiently out of the way, as we have seen with the Echinocystis, as soon as the tendril comes in its revolving course to this point, it stiffens and straightens itself, and thus rising vertically up passes over the obstacle in an admirable manner.

All tendrils are sensitive, but in various degrees, to contact with an object, and curve toward the touched side. With several plants, a single

---

* Climbing Plants, p. 99.　　† Ibid.　　‡ Ibid. p. 105.

touch, so slight as just to move the highly flexible tendril, is enough to induce curvature. Passiflora gracilis possesses the most sensitive tendrils which I have observed. A bit of platina wire, one-fiftieth of a grain in weight, gently placed on the concave point, caused a tendril to become hooked."* "Asa Gray also observed movement in the tendrils of the Cucurbitaceous genus, Sicyos, in 30 seconds. The tendrils of some other plants, when lightly rubbed, moved in a few minutes. * * * It makes no difference what sort of object a tendril touches, with the remarkable exception of other tendrils and drops of water."† "With most tendrils the leaves or basal part is either not at all sensitive, or sensitive only to prolonged contact. We thus see that the sensitiveness of tendrils is a special and localized capacity."‡ Twining plants, when they come into contact with a stick, curl round it invariably in the direction of their revolving movement; but tendrils curl indifferently to either side, in accordance with the position of the stick and the side which is first touched."§

Here, then, we have in the plant sensitiveness extending to the most delicate touch, an immediate adjustment of motions to it, a discrimination between objects, so that another tendril or a drop of water are not allowed to occupy time and waste energy, and a very remarkable sensitiveness to the light, not as an agent in growth merely, but as a guide to the tendril in finding its point of attach-

* Climbing Plants, p. 171.   † Ibid. p. 172.   ‡ Ibid. p. 173.
§ Ibid

ment. The conduct of the tendril when it has obtained or failed to obtain its object is not less
remarkably fitted to changeable external conditions.
" Tendrils soon after catching a support grow much
stronger and thicker, and sometimes more durable
to a wonderful degree ; and this shows how much
their internal tissues must be changed. Occasionally it is the part which is wound round a support
which chiefly becomes thicker and stronger ; I have
seen, for instance, this part of a tendril of Bignonia
aequinoctialis twice as thick and rigid as the free
basal part. Tendrils which have caught nothing
soon shrink and wither." *   " The tendrils and internodes of Ampelopsis have little or no power of
revolving ; the tendrils are but little sensitive to contact ; their hooked extremities cannot seize their
objects ; they will not even clasp a stick, unless in
extreme need of a support ; but they turn from the
light to the dark, and, spreading out their branches
in contact with any nearly flat surface, develop discs.
These adhere by the secretion of some cement to a
wall or even to a polished surface. The rapid
development of these adherent discs is one of the
most remarkable peculiarities possessed by any
tendril." †

There are, then, a half-dozen of very special actions and of marked changes in constitution by
which a tendril performs its offices. Failing in a
first function, it substitutes a second ; failing in
this it drops away. Once attached it constructs its
spirals and strengthens its substance, that it may

---

* Climbing Plants, p. 175.   † Ibid. p. 179.

do its work thoroughly well. Unable to clasp its support, it plants the tip of the tendril as a disc, and maintains the upward growth. It goes at its labor in each instance with apt and fresh resources. " It has often been vaguely asserted that plants are distinguished from animals by not having the power of movement. It should rather be said that plants acquire and display this power only where it is of some advantage to them ; this being of comparatively rare occurrence, as they are affixed to the ground, and food is brought to them by the air and rains. We see how high in the scale of organization a plant may rise, when we look at one of the more perfect tendril-bearers. It first places its tendrils ready for action, as a polypus places its tentacula. If the tendril be displaced, it is acted on by the force of gravity and rights itself. It is acted on by the light and bends toward or from it, or disregards it, whichever may be most advantageous. During several days the tendrils, or internodes, or both, spontaneously revolve with a steady motion. The tendril strikes some object, and quickly coils round and firmly grasps it. In the course of some hours it contracts into a spire, dragging up the stem and forming an excellent spring. All movements now cease. By growth the tissues soon become wonderfully strong and durable. The tendril has done its work, and has done it in an admirable manner." *

Our purpose in bringing these facts together is simply to emphasize the extent of the organic au-

* Climbing Plants, p. 206

tomatic processes we reach in the vegetable kingdom before we touch the animal kingdom, and, by
general consent, before we reach consciousness.
We have merely hinted at the decisive plastic power
which belongs to the higher plants, and at some of
the more striking adaptations which it reaches. Of
the great variety of its manifestations on this plane
we have said nothing ; of the many ways in which
it constructs and guides a plant for its own specific
ends.   The plane is one, but the plastic powers at
work upon it are many.   Our interpretation of the
animal kingdom in which the plane itself is slowly
shifted will be greatly modified by the highly developed organic structures which we have found below
it.   To be sure these plants are in no sense in
direct line with animal life, but organic functions
remain none the less essentially the same as a
form of development.   The organic forces which
reach in the vegetable such remarkable results with
no nervous system, may, where such an instrument
is present, mount higher and do very much more
with no enlargement of function by an indwelling
intelligence.

These powers of construction and adaptation in
the vegetable are also transmitted. The seed, which
may lie dormant so long, and which shows so little
organic material beyond the accumulation of nutriment, transmits, like the ovum, specific qualities.
There is here, however, a remarkable difference.
The seed, as of the apple, may drop in growth the
qualities which make the variety, and assume with
advance or more frequently with retrogression new

ones. At the same time each section of the wood of the apple in grafting, though fed and thoroughly flooded by alien sap, retains, in fruiting its own specific qualities. While there is, then, a law of descent in plants the counterpart of that in animals, the facts being no more inscrutable in the one case than in the other, there is in plants a peculiar, almost a capricious, manifestation of this law favoring artificial propagation as opposed to natural descent. Any theory of heredity should go quite back to the vegetable kingdom, and cover its phenomena as well as those of the animal kingdom. If we can in one case dispense with the mediation of peculiar forces, with gemmules and physiological units, we can do so equally well in the other. If gemmules are present in the apple-tree, they are present in its wood, not specialized for transmission, as they are not present in its seed, its most concentrate living product, highly specialized for this very purpose. Moreover, they are present in the wood, the relatively dead element, rather than in the sap, the relatively living element, since it is the wood that remains the same in the graft, while the nourishing sap is rapidly altered. If the sap alone of the twig were charged with gemmules, these would be largely displaced with other gemmules, before it became a branch and brought forth fruit. But if gemmules are not the media of transfer, if they are present neither in its seed nor in its wood, there is no reason why we should think them present in man, since the law of inheritance is distinctly one law from the very beginning. There is a rehearsal in outline in the vegetable kingdom of those organic processes in whose more complete development animal life is the second stage. Not less certainly are the lower powers to be studied and measured on their own plane and then carried up into the higher organism for fresh manifestations there, than is the food of the animal to be recognized as first the food of the plant and the material of its structure. The laws of life are the same from the beginning to the end, with such enlargement and modifications as new conditions require. We are not to accept the new element before it is called for, nor deny its value when it is manifestly present ; nor having admitted it are we to bear it surreptitiously back to explain the old facts. We start with an inscrutable element, that element may well go with us to the end. Our knowledge lies in reducing it to its simplest terms, in noting the order and stages of its introduction, and in tracing through their successive steps and relations freely open to us that great structure, the Cosmos, physical and spiritual, which has sprung up out of them. The productive steps of the Divine method are our thoughts. As each higher organization, passing up to human intelligence, rests in uses and powers on all that lies below it, we must understand it, first, in its common foundation-terms, and, secondly, in its differentia, in that which it itself brings to the organic kingdom for its enlargement.

CHAPTER IV.

THE NERVOUS SYSTEM.

THE first function of the nervous system is to disseminate the stimuli which are productive of motions in organic beings, and to hasten their action. We have seen that motion under an external irritant belongs to plants, but this motion is relatively restricted and usually tardy. The lower forms of animal life, in which no nervous system is apparent, also move under provocation, but the movement is more simple, less definite and decided than in more advanced organisms. Definiteness, extension and decision of movement are the results of the widely and rapidly transferred energies of a nervous system.

A second office of the system is to aid in the specialization of functions and organs. This system is itself such a specialization. It also combines and harmonizes distinct organs in strictly concurrent action. Indeed this system would seem to be a primary condition of union and successful activity in a being of various, complicated and closely inter-dependent parts. Though, as a fact, considerable complexity and entire harmony of action are obtained without this system, the variety of functions and their immediateness of inter-action are greatly increased in connection with it. It transfers stimuli, combines stimuli, and so distributes them as to call forth various and harmonious action throughout the organic being in a wonderful way. A nervous system is thus itself a specific structure, set apart to a specific office, and also a means to the extension of specialization in all directions, by uniting each function with every other.

A third office of a nervous system is the multiplication of the kinds of stimuli. It is not merely mechanical contact that is operative under it ; but, through special organs, light, sound, flavors and odors become sharp and decisive incentives. Something of this enlargement of sensibility belongs even to the plant. It responds in movement to the light, and seems to be affected by conditions of fertility and moisture at a slight remove from it. Yet these anticipatory facts present but a faint image of the varied sensitiveness of a nervous system, when developed in the higher animals into special organs. This system not only combines the animal into one life and experience within itself, it gives great extension and delicacy to its relations to surrounding conditions, to its environment. These interior and exterior dependences are farther enlarged by the variety of sensations which report the condition of every organ and portion of the body, sensations to which there is no definite limit either in their own nature or in the facts which they disclose.

The highest function of the nervous system, one which comes only at a late period and very slowly to it, but at length constitutes its primary office, is to furnish the conditions of a conscious life, and carry that life as a controlling power through the entire organism. Consciousness in its lower forms seems simply to minister to farther ease and accuracy of adjustment in organic actions, and to secure increasing completeness of correspondence with external circumstances. It is simply a new term in the extension of an equilibration already very perfect. In its higher forms, however, it comes to assume the attitude of a preëminent life, and compels every other activity to minister to its new spiritual functions.

We are chiefly interested in the nervous structure because of these its altered relations to consciousness, but we must none the less understand its organic offices before we can comprehend its intellectual ones; since the latter grow out of and rest upon the former. Before we venture to indicate the steps of psychological development we will give, in a most general way, the parts which compose the nervous system, its various gradations, their relations to each other, and their order of development. We shall take no notice of exceptional facts which do not modify the force of general truths ; nor of the many phases which intervene between typical forms ; nor of the innumerable varieties which surround them. Our purpose is more simple, an indication of the line of development and its salient positions. It is not the windings of the

river, but its sources and directions, the territory
which feeds it, and its débouchure which interest
us.

The essential facts of the simplest nervous system are nerves and a ganglion ; this as a centre of
reception and distribution, and those as lines of
communication. Such a system we find in the
Ascidians. These two parts are distinguished in
position, structure, and function. The nerve-fibres
are themselves distinguished by functions into af-
ferent and efferent, according as they bear a stimulus inward to a ganglion, or an impulse outward
from it. The relation of these first terms of a nervous system to each other is as direct and mechanical as that of mail lines by which letters are sent
to a distributing office, and thence scattered to
their destination. · Of the nature of the energy
transferred along the nerves, or of the method of
its distribution by the ganglion, we know very
little. The double office of the nerves is due perhaps wholly to their points of origin and termina-
tion ; as their structure seems identical. The affe-
rent nerves start in surfaces of sensation, general
or special, and terminate in ganglia to which they
transmit the impulses received. The efferent
nerves have a distinct origin in the same ganglia,
and terminate in muscles or organs to which they
transfer the stimulus as redirected by the ganglia.
The one set, therefore, acts in reference to the
other as a secondary or return track.

The simplest form of a nervous system is that of
a single ganglion, with its direct nervous commu-

nications. Such a system is sufficient for the first function mentioned. It gives extension and decision to movement. The Tunicata may be cited as showing this primary form. "A single ganglion lies between the base of the two funnels through which water is taken and discharged." The second step is a more familiar one. In it several ganglia, each with its own nervous connections, are united by internuncial nerves so that the stimuli of all are combined and harmonized in action. This is the simplest extension of the first principle, but is a type of a large portion of nervous structure. In animals, like the Radiata, in which a circular symmetry and equality of parts prevail, this form of a nervous system is especially harmonious with the general structure. In the starfish, a single ganglion near the mouth stands in connection with each ray, and these being united with each other, the impulse of each is extended to all. Or these ganglia are continuous and constitute a ring of vesicular matter surrounding the mouth and sending filaments to each ray.

This type of structure performs, certainly, the first and second functions. It diffuses motion, and promotes specialization by more extensively combining distinct parts into one whole. It may also add the third function, that of varying and multiplying the forms of stimuli. Thus, the Radiata may have ocelli at the extremities of the rays, and the nerves passing from them be farther supported by minute ganglia of their own.

The Articulata, like the Radiata, are remarkable

for a repetition of similar parts, though these parts are now placed longitudinally. The segments of the Articulata instead of coming round in a circle, which gives no distinction of anterior and posterior, no beginning or end, are arranged in a line, and so start with a head and end with a tail. Thus, however extended may be their multiplication of like parts, they disclose these leading animal features. The centipede is a good illustration. The nervous system of the Articulata is in accordance with this their structure. It consists of a series of similar ganglia with their filaments ; these ganglia, composed of two lobes, being united by a double nervous cord. The twin ganglia closely correspond to each other, and are evenly distributed one to each segment. "The more alike the different segments the more equal are the ganglia."* As the Articulata have a distinct head, so also the nervous ganglia of the head show a distinct relation, and a preëminence over other ganglia according as the head is more or less fully developed. As the nervous cord is ventral, not dorsal, it closes anteriorly below the œsophagus and back of the mouth with the sub-œsophageal ganglia. The two filaments of the cord enclose the œsophagus, and unite above it in the cephalic ganglia. These ganglia are usually larger than those of the segments, are the seats of special senses, and have an independent connection with the inferior centres. In addition to the direct connection of the several ganglia as successive links in one chain, a distinct line of nervous

* Carpenter's Comparative Physiology, p. 663.

fibre extends from the cephalic ganglia backward, giving off branches to each member of the series. The cephalic ganglia are thus put in more immediate control of all movements, and we have a third principle introduced into the nervous system, that of centralization, or cephalization. Cephalization, however, may be said to involve two points; first, a predominant influence of the cephalic ganglia; second, a gathering more and more of the ganglia into the head. These three stages of nervous construction, single ganglia, united ganglia, subordinate and concentrated ganglia, carry us up to the sub-kingdom of the Vertebrata.

In proportion as development advances in the Articulata is the head specialized, and do its ganglia become more supreme in function and more numerous. In the earth-worm, on the other hand, the several ganglia are comparatively merged in a continuous cord extending the whole length of the body. As, passing from this type of absolute uniformity, the segments of the body are more specialized, and so more diverse, their ganglia are modified in size, some of them are combined, some of them are suppressed, and the spaces between them are changed, In the insects, the highest class in this sub-kingdom, the cephalic ganglia are greatly enlarged, are closely united to the sub-œsophageal ganglia or first ganglia of the trunk, and take them more immediately under their influence. The second ganglia of the trunk retire to the middle of the thorax; the third quite disappear; the fourth and fifth coalesce; the sixth and seventh are obliterated; while the remaining ganglia are much smaller in proportion to the rest.*

Thus, the nervous system in the insect at once conforms to the new structure by a concentration of offices. It loses its regularity, and is adapted to a more varied, and more thoroughly harmonized activity of the several portions of the body. It is especially gathered up in the head and thorax, the former the seat of special senses, the latter of the locomotive apparatus. In this concentration in insects of nervous energy in the head, we have a preparation for the remarkable instincts of a portion of that order ; and in the great increase of nervous energy in the thorax, a provision for the rapid and powerful flight of many of them. While there is this general correspondence of the nervous system to the new powers developed, the surprising instincts of certain families, as of the ant, bee, and spider, are not sufficiently explained by these modifications. In the spider there is a yet further gathering together of the nervous ganglia towards the head. The abdominal, thoracic and sub-œsophageal ganglia are fused into one mass, and this is brought in close connection with the cerebral ganglia. †

The symmetry which belongs to the Radiata and Articulata disappears in the Mollusca. The relation of parts is less uniform and harmonious in this branch of the animal kingdom than in any other. In keeping with this fact, the nervous ganglia are

* Carpenter's Comparative Physiology, p. 672.
† Popular Science Monthly, 9th vol. p. 710,

more scattered, and vary more in their relations than in the other sub-kingdoms.

The typical arrangement in this division, which means even here nothing more than the midway form, includes, first, the cephalic ganglia which may lie as a pair on either side of the œsophagus, or be united as a bilobed mass above it ; secondly, the sub-œsophageal or pedal ganglia lying just below the œsophagus ; and, thirdly, the posterior or parieto-splanchnic ganglia. The posterior ganglia are frequently represented by two pairs of ganglia, separate in position and divided in office. One pair is connected with the respiratory organs, and is termed the branchial ganglia ; the other is united to the mantle, and is called the pallial ganglia. · This pair is sometimes united with the branchial ganglia, at other times carried forward to the pedal ganglia.

As the range of development is very great in the Mollusca, this midway type of nervous structure, composed of ganglia quite distinct in position and office, and proximately equal in value, though united in one system, fails to represent the many varieties of arrangement above and below it. We have already mentioned the Tunicata as possessing but one ganglion. Many of the Mollusca are headless, and the ganglia which gather about the mouth, above and below the œsophagus, are proportionally secondary in importance. The supra-œso-phageal ganglia, corresponding to the cephalic ganglia, are entirely wanting in the chiton ; and in the oyster the posterior ganglia are superior in size to the anterior ganglia.

In the cuttle-fish, which belongs to the highest
division of Mollusca, the cephalic ganglia are large,
and the other ganglia are drawn forward in close
connection with them, beneath the œsophagus.
In this highest branch of the sub-kingdom, the supremacy of the cephalic ganglia is fully shown, and
also the concentration of ganglia incident to discriminating, energetic, and united action.

In the Vertebrata we start from the very beginning with one general arrangement uniformly maintained; the variety being found in the different
degrees of development in different ganglia. This
variety, however, has a large range, passing from
the entire absence of cephalic ganglia up to their
complete supremacy in man. This uniform arrangement is a spinal cord, in place of a ventral
cord, and, to replace the scattered ganglia of the
ventral cord, an encephalon. This is composed of
many ganglia, with great variety in different animals in their relative sizes, but all compactly placed
in the head. The foundation of this system, containing the ganglia and connections analogous to
lower systems, is first, the spinal cord—this in an
extreme case may be the only member—and, secondly, "its anterior prolongation known as the medulla oblongata, and the sensory ganglia in still farther continuation of the series." On this are erected,
to this fundamental automatic mechanism are added,
the cerebellum and the cerebrum; "to which," says
Dr. Carpenter, "nothing distinctly analogous can
be detected in any of the inferior classes." The
motor and sensory ganglia, themselves large and

varied, which represent corresponding ganglia in lower forms of life, are wonderfully supported and within limits controlled by these large ganglia the cerebellum and, in the higher classes of the sub-kingdom, by the much larger and overshadowing ganglia, the cerebrum. The cerebellum does not seem to be the seat of any conscious activity, but a means of coördinating the numerous impressions and the very complicated actions which belong to the higher animals. It is a motor reverberatory centre which fulfils its office alike automatically, whether the impulse be conscious or unconscious, voluntary or involuntary, in its origin.* The extent of the coördination incident to the superior forms of life is indicated by the relative size of these ganglia. The cerebrum is regarded as the exclusive seat of consciousness in the higher animals. " The destruction of the cerebral hemispheres, by annihilating sensation, ideation, volition, and intelligence in general, reduces the animal to the condition of a complex machine."† The cerebrum is thus the specialized organ of consciousness, and so in the Vertebrata of intelligence.

In the Amphioxus or " brainless fishes," the lowest members of this division of the animal kingdom, the cerebellum and the cerebrum are both wanting. In the lower Vertebrata, these ganglia are quite inferior to the sensory and motor ganglia. As we pass upward, there is a constant though not a uniform increase in the size of the higher ganglia, till, in man, they have attained not only a superior,

* Ferrier's Functions of the Brain, p. 86.　† Ibid. p. 124.

but a preëminent position. The relative importance
of these seats of conscious life, and of that coördination to which the voluntary life owes its chief
efficiency, is made up of many things.   It is a preëminence in man which may seem to suffer slight
disparagement in one or another particular, but becomes complete and undeniable when all points of
view are combined.   The cerebral superiority of
man is like his superiority in the special senses
He may be greatly outstripped in some one perception, as by the vulture in vision, or by the hound
in scent, but when the whole circle of the senses
is considered, their adaptation to his specific purposes, their great enlargement by the judgments
of experience, and their thorough support by his
rational and voluntary constitution, we see that
man is in this direction wonderfully superior to any
animal.

In absolute size the brain of man falls below
that of the elephant and the whale; but this fact
is not very significant when we remember the comparatively coarse structure of these animals, their
very great bulk, and the consequent expenditure of
physical force, to be sustained by a nervous system
somewhat corresponding in energy.   The fact, then,
of only a slightly greater weight of brain in these
large and not unsagacious animals serves to make
manifest man's superiority.   But in relative size,
also, that is, in its weight as compared with the
weight of the body, the brain of other animals sur-
passes that of man.   The brain, when fully developed, constitutes in man about one-fiftieth of the

entire body. In some birds it constitutes one-twelfth. The range in the relative size of the brain in animals is very great. In the star-fish it is 1 to 8915; in the goose 1 to 3600. The ratio is more favorable in the smaller animals than in the larger ones of the same class. The smaller birds are some of them remarkable for the great relative size of the brain. In the tomtit it is 1 to 12; in the canary bird 1 to 14; in the Arctic sparrow 1 to 11.* The reason for this unusual size in small birds would seem to be obvious, though there is no corresponding increase in intelligence. The activity, the muscular effort, in this entire class, is very great, and should be accompanied with a relatively large nervous development. But this muscular activity is usually greater in the smaller than in the larger birds. Moreover, the organic power dependent on the nervous power must be relatively much greater in a small bird like the Arctic sparrow, than in a larger one like the eider-duck. To maintain a uniform temperature in that little furnace of life encased in the breast of a snow-bunting ; to so heat the blood that it shall be driven in genial currents through legs hardly as large as grass-stalks ; reach unchilled the extremities of the tiny claws, and return thence to the body unfrozen, while the cheerful bird is darting through the sharp northern blast, or resting on icy stems, or running on the snow, imply a wonderful energy of life, and may well call for a large nervous development.

* Journal of Mental and Nervous Diseases, Vol. I. No. 1.— *Hammond.*

It is doubtless true also that in small animals, what we may call the first terms of the nervous system being necessarily present, the ganglia all complete, the size of the nervous system becomes thereby relatively greater than in larger animals. In these there is an additional expansion of nerves, but no new ganglia ; and as the nerves help to sustain them in energy there is no occasion as these lengthen for a corresponding increase of the central ganglia. Development in the nervous system has another factor beside size ; it is not simply additive, but implies also a more perfect coördination of existing parts. This view is sustained by the fact that the brain is relatively larger at birth than later in life. Growth involves the mastery of the organs already present in this case, more than their increase. In a rat-terrier at birth, the ratio of the brain to the body, as given by Prof. Wilder, was .054 ; in a second specimen, six months of age, it was .028. In a shepherd dog, a few days old, it was .028 ; in one six weeks old it was .021. A much greater contrast, however, is shown in the same tables between larger and smaller breeds.* Thus in the Newfoundland dog the ratio was .003 ; in the bull and cur, .003 ; and in the St. Bernard, .002. Yet these are especially intelligent varieties. Imperfect tables of the relative sizes of the brain in other animals, chiefly Carnivora, indicate, though less clearly, the same relations. It is probable that domestic animals owe more to training, and less to

---

* Anatomical Papers, by Burt G. Wilder, p. 235.

original size and primary functions, than do wild animals.

Another contrast in weight is that between the gray and the white matter in the same system. A preponderance of white matter indicates a corresponding muscular vigor, and a preponderance of the gray matter a more complete concentration of functions, an increase of the conscious and voluntary life. In this respect man is preëminent. Says Dr. Hammond, in the article referred to: "Unless regard is paid to this point, we should certainly fall into serious errors in determining the relation existing between the mind and the nervous system; but having it in view, the connection is at once clear and well-defined, there being no exception to the law that the mental development is in direct proportion to the amount of the gray matter entering into the composition of the nervous system of any animal of any kind whatever. * * * When we inquire into the absolute and relative amount of the gray tissue, man stands preëminent; it is to this fact that he owes the great mental development which places him so far above all other living beings."

This relation of the entire brain in its size to its composite offices; the relation in the size of one or other of its parts to its special offices; and the proportion of the vesicular to its fibrous material, according as mental or physical vigor is to be exerted, find various illustration. Thus the porpoise, an exceedingly active animal, in a dense medium, has a large weight of brain, with no preponderance of gray matter. In the torpedo, the medulla oblongata is equal to all the rest of the brain, but this is the centre which gives rise to its peculiar electric shock. So also special senses are developed into an unusual relative importance only in connection with a corresponding size of their appropriate ganglia. The sensory and optic lobes in many of the lower animals are relatively very large. In the carp, the optic lobes are much superior to the cerebral hemispheres. While this may not indicate any unusual power of vision, it does show that the automatic action of the animal turns largely on this sense. It points to the source of stimuli and the seat of reflex action.

Another point of difference in the cerebrum in man, indicating a decidedly superior functional activity in this organ, are the number and depth of convolutions. In this respect there is steady development as we pass up along the higher members of the Vertebrata, till, in man, we reach a maximum. These convolutions, with the dipping of the *pia mater* into the substance of the brain, are very significant. The surface of the brain is correspondingly enlarged, and the enveloping membrane bears with it, in its abundant blood-vessels, the blood that enriches the organ and stimulates its activity. In reference to the power of the hemispheres, they indicate what extent of cellular surface does in the lungs. While the exact pattern of these convolutions is not of moment, " other things being equal, a greater number and depth of fissures indicate a greater mental or bodily power, and the actual number of fissures has a general functional significance, analogous to coils of intestines or corrugations of mucous membranes."*

The office of the cerebrum in man, and its superiority in that office, find decided expression in these combined facts, without our being able to define the exact value that attaches to any of them. In the cerebellum and cerebrum, the gray matter is exterior to the white matter, overlying it as a heavy enveloping surface. In ordinary ganglia the arrangement is the reverse of this. The enclosed gray matter at the centre of the white fibrous lines of communication seems simply to combine and redirect the forces that are at play upon it. The greatly extended and external gray matter of the cerebrum seems to indicate that, as the seat of consciousness, it is not merely an interior point of intersection and dispersion, among impulses already completely realized, but that it is able from its manifold convolutions to send forth the supreme and relatively independent impulses of thought and volition. A kindred significance attaches to the fact that it is superinduced on the ordinary sensory and motor ganglia, and, with no independent connections with the outside world, receives its external incentives through them, and sends its own impulses back upon them. These subordinate ganglia, as seen elsewhere in the animal kingdom, are quite capable of the lower forms of coördination, and do not require the support of the superior ganglia, except as a conscious and voluntary life intervenes. It is

* Anatomical Papers, by Burt G. Wilder, p. 247.

not probable that the cerebrum is simply a second massive reverberating organ, brought in to extend and enforce the functional activities that lie below it. This the cerebellum may well enough be in connection with the greatly enlarged coördination of higher life. But if this life itself, a new and measurably independent power, has no existence, a second and much larger organ of coördination in lower functions can hardly be called for.

The relations of the cerebrum, taken in connection with the faculties of man, seem plainly to express the fact that these hemispheres give us the first term on the material side in the inexplicable union of matter and mind, that by and through them the powers of thought find their way among the forces of matter. These ganglia have thus a functional office proportioned to their preëminence. The overshadowing power of the rational life in man is boldly expressed in the physical relations or language of these hemispheres, uniting to cover and crown all the ganglia of functional and animal life beneath them.

There is very much special knowledge which we may well wish to add to our very general knowledge of the nervous system in animals and man. We are sure of its chief functions; we are fairly certain of the offices of its primary portions, but we have very little knowledge of the precise way in which its work is done, or of the interdependence of the several parts of any ganglia. It is easy to multiply mechanical illustrations, but the combination and dispersion of stimuli at the simplest nervous

centre are beyond their powers of explanation.
There is still a decided tendency to divide up in
functions the larger ganglia, more especially the
cerebrum, and to assign a definite duty to each portion of this elaborate organ. This effort has recently met, especially in the hands of Mr. Ferrier,
with some success. While it still remains true that
these ganglia, as the instruments of mind, work in a
way wholly inscrutable, and that one portion can
largely replace other portions of the hemispheres,
it has also been made plain that the fibres passing
to and from it have specialized sensor and motor
functions. This fact puts the cerebrum in harmony
with the nervous mechanism that lies below it, and
seems sufficiently established by vivisection and
pathology. Yet philosophy and science also, at
least in a portion of its special laborers, incline to the
opinion that the cerebrum is, in some indivisible
way, the organ of mind ; that intellectual activity is
pervasive and controlling in the brain as in the rest
of the body. " I am more and more inclined to
think,"* says Prof. Wilder, " that a cerebral hemisphere acts as a unit, either singly or with its fellow."

What, then, is the probable relation of these two
facts, that inquiry on the one side confirms a division of offices in reference to the body, extending to
every part of the cerebrum ; and that every effort to
locate the powers of mind miscarries ? Is it not a
relation, the exact counterpart of the relation between the body and the plastic powers we term

* Anatomical Papers, by Burt G. Wilder, p. 247.

life? Distinct organs and separate functions neither subdivide nor localize the presiding tendency, but leave it fully at work in every part of the body.

We are to bear distinctly in mind the strictly organic dependence of the cerebrum on the remainder of the nervous system, remembering that it is by these connections alone that it can be the organ of mind. Completeness and precision of relation are the physical preparation for perfect control. " The cerebral hemispheres form each a sort of hollow shell, enclosing and enveloping the great basal ganglia, the inner walls being formed in great measure by the hollow cone of medullary fibres radiating in all directions from these structures."* This corona radiata, with its immense assemblage of diverging fibres, covered and contained by the gray matter of the cerebrum, as by a dome, unites the entire inner surface of the hemispheres with the sensor and motor mechanism of life, the powerful coördinating ganglia that lie below them. As every office of communication and interchange through this inferior portion of the nervous system is specific, with its own circuits, this fact necessitates the same division of service in the cerebrum. The general regions through which particular sensor or motor tracks take their way, or the points at which they originate, have doubtless been determined by Ferrier with proximate correctness. Till we reach the cerebrum, we have the quasi-mechanical features of the nervous system, and these cer-

* Functions of the Brain, p. 9.

tainly ought to complete themselves through its every member. Any sudden interruption would destroy their entire significance, and put it out of harmony with its instruments.

The exterior layers of the cerebrum, with their increasingly minute vesicular structure as we approach the surface, with their extended convolutions,—the last, highest, and fullest term in the perfected nervous system—still remain, however, the single condition, the undivided organ, of conscious life in its supreme unity. The subtile light of thought plays an ambient flame over the cerebrum, or, unlocking its tense forces, sends an impulse through it in a way as inscrutable as mind itself. We travel by physical connections and causal dependencies safely enough till we reach this boundary land, but here vision fails us, and we are left on the verge of the material world without a single outlying premise. The general mastery of the mind, its many instruments, its local developments in them and by them, remain our ultimate truths. Its own manifestations we may struggle to overlook or to degrade in character, but to the rational eye they have always been, and will remain, the language of free thought, the traces of spiritual power.

Ferrier, like others, whose attention is primarily directed to physical connections, who approach mind through matter, is ready to push his conclusions beyond his data. He says, "We have reason for believing that there is, in company with all our mental processes, *an unbroken material succession.* From the ingress of a sensation, to the outgoing responses in action, the mental succession is not for an instant dissevered from a physical succession."*

"The primordial elements of the volitional acts of the infant, and also of the adult, are capable of being reduced in ultimate physiological analysis to reaction between the centres of sensation and those of motion."†

This is a conclusion, in its bearing on our highest spiritual powers, in advance of his experiments by its entire length. To the completeness of the sensory and motor circuits even in their passage through the cerebrum he is entitled, to the assertion that our conscious and voluntary activities are included in these circuits he is not entitled. The same circuits lie in lower ganglia and are often completed in them. It is in the cerebrum alone, as Ferrier allows, that a new element enters, that of consciousness. The very purpose of the hemispheres seems to be the introduction into automatic circuits of voluntary and conscious control. To make the action in these superadded ganglia identical with it in the lower ganglia is to rob them of their significance. Indeed, when this is accomplished, when the involuntary has by repetition been transformed into the automatic, the circuit is narrowed once more, and the series passed over to the lower ganglia in which it can be completed as " an unbroken, material succession." In other words, when we have an unbroken material succession, we have no longer occasion for the intervention of the cere-

---

* Functions of the Brain, p. 256. † Ibid. p. 282

brum. The very intent of this organ is in some inscrutable way to introduce the new element of conscious activity, and modify the material circuit
by it.

The destruction of the cerebrum interferes only
with voluntary action, and hence affects different
forms of life in very different degrees, according to
the extent to which organic action is modified and
sustained by voluntary effort. In man, two large
ganglia, the optici thalami and the còrpora striata,
are found in the closest connection with the cerebrum, ready to receive and maintain the coördinations established by it, or to restore them again to
it for its further modification. " The more the control of the limbs depends in the first instance, and
continues to be dependent, on voluntary acquisition,
the more does the destruction of the cortical motor
centres cause paralysis of movement. Hence in
man and the monkey, in whom· volition is predominant, and automaticity plays only a subordinate
part in the motor activities, destruction of the motor centres of the cortex causes paralysis of a very
marked character. In proportion, however, as
movements at first requiring volitional education,
tend to become organized or rendered automatic,
the less are they affected by injury to the cortical
centres. Hence, in the dog, in which the acquisition,
of the control of the limbs is speedy, the destruction of the cortical centres produces a much less
marked effect."* Still less are the actions of the
rabbit and the frog modified by the loss of the

* Functions of the Brain, p. 213.

cerebrum. The plain conclusions then are, that
automatic action, or the "unbroken material succession" of which Ferrier speaks, is the characteristic of lower ganglia, and that the very preëminence of the cerebrum is that it breaks in on this
material sequence with new and controlling terms.
These facts involve two kinds of circuits, one with
and one without the voluntary element. To affirm
the identity of the two in their leading characteristics is to lose the key of explanation.

Accident and disease, issuing in a sensible loss
of the substance of the cerebrum, yet with no well
defined effect on the powers of mind, indicate that
our intellectual faculties are not local functions.
Having given the celebrated case in which a bar of
iron was driven quite through the top of the head
with no serious injury following to the mind of the
patient after recovery, Ferrier proceeds : "Numerous other cases might be cited where considerable
portions of the brain-substance, protruding through
fractures of the skull, have been removed by sur-
geons without causing evil results or apparent mental deficiency."*

Aphasia, occasioned by a local disturbance of
the brain, leads us to the same conclusion. The
patient is embarrassed in uttering words, and not
in the mental conceptions which accompany them.
The organs of speech yield the wrong sounds. The
mechanical, the automatic circuit has been broken,
and the mind, though in full power, cannot send
through the impulse of articulation. This fact ex-

* Functions of the Brain, p. 126.

hibits clearly, in a single direction, what is true in all directions ; the mind lets drop in a blind way its purposes on the mechanism below ; and is then at its mercy for their fulfilment.   That the circuit can be checked, and the conscious conception remain, indicates the radical division of the two.

Ferrier immediately proceeds to make statements inconsistent with his first assertion of an unbroken material succession.   " The brain as an organ of motion and sensation, or presentative consciousness, is a single organ composed of two halves; the brain as an organ of ideation, representative consciousness, is a dual organ, each hemisphere complete in itself.   When one hemisphere is removed or destroyed by disease, motion and sensation are abolished unilaterally, but mental operations are still capable of being carried on in their completeness through the agency of the one hemisphere."*   But if the mind can be loosened from all specific physical connections in one hemisphere without loss, by a transfer of paralysis it might have been loosened in the same manner in the other hemisphere with the same results ; and this proves that the mind has no necessary specific connections, that it is not involved in any of its powers as a fixed term in any circuits, but is dependent in a general variable way on all circuits as volitional instruments.   The only merit of the materialistic view is that it involves the mental element exactly and constantly in the physical one. If it yields the least at this point, the whole ground

* Functions of the Brain, p. 257.

8

drops from under it. The brain cannot be a single motor and sensory organ, and a dual conscious one, unless we are willing to admit that conscious states are not in exact correspondence with physical ones.

Again Ferrier speaks of the power of concentrating attention, and of inhibitory centres : " The inhibitory centres are not equally developed or educated in all, nor are they equally developed in the same individual in respect to particular tendencies to action." * He even proceeds to localize these centres in " the frontal lobes of the brain." This language can hardly have a meaning under the doctrine of unbroken material successions. Such successions have their sufficient and final physical causes ; they can neither be intensified by attention nor arrested by inhibition. Attention and inhibition are not physical connections but spiritual powers. Successions may concur with each other, or contravene each other, stimuli may add or subtract themselves in the final result ; but mind alone can hasten or delay action, can command or forbid it. Ferrier has expelled this supreme power only to revive it again under the new title, " centres of inhibition." The scientist is fond of doing this. He is quick to accuse the psychologist of deceiving himself with words ; but the illusion is more general than the accusation implies. Words which belong to the mind only are first carried over in a figurative way to the brain, and then shortly regarded as the literal

* Functions of the Brain, p. 283.

equivalents of intellectual facts. Thus we bridge the chasm between matter and mind with a word-structure, which has secure foundations at neither extremity ; we turn the facts of the brain into figures of speech, and we know nothing of their correspondence with the mental states they are made to represent. Centres of inhibition mean volition, and must either restore volition or quite fail of their purpose.

It must always be the supreme objection to physical coherences as explanations of mental processes that they do not expound, but annihilate, the phenomena offered to them. Mental connections and mental activities disappear before them as the impotent shadows of physical forces. The integrity of the very process of thought by which we construct the theory is taken away by the theory itself. There is certainly as yet no proof, and there hardly can be any proof, that every idea, purpose, feeling is the product of some specific state of special vesicles of the brain. Phrenology, as a local division and distribution of mental processes throughout the cerebrum, has been losing ground from the beginning, but this supposition as a localizing tendency goes much farther. Under this view, any injury to the brain should carry with it as distinct a mischief as an accident in a toy shop. The experiments which are thought to look to such a conclusion are inexpressibly coarse and inadequate for their purpose. We cannot touch so deftly and harmoniously the ultimate vesicles of the brain as to secure their normal activity, nor could we, if this were possible, read the cipher in which their functional action is written. Yet this assumption of an exact equivalence between a physical and a mental state, wholly in advance as it is of our knowledge, is involved in the confident assertion of unbroken material successions in the cerebrum. The logical outcome of this statement is the complete subordination of mind to matter.

Our most general conclusions, those in which all opinions best harmonize, are our safest ones; and the views that we have to offer involve alone these first principles. We have traced the growth and the offices of the nervous system sufficiently for our purposes. We started with it as a very simple instrument brought in to aid and further organic relations already established. We traced a few of the steps of development by which, on the one hand, it has become the avenue of very varied and extended impulses, and on the other has coördinated them into correspondingly complicated action. We observed the increasing unity keeping pace with the increasing complexity of these processes, a unity which expresses and establishes itself in cephalization. We saw, as the last and highest function of the nervous system, a new life by the introduction of consciousness superinduced on the old life, yet precisely in the line of its expansion. We saw also by the slow growth of the hemispheres a special instrument set apart for this supreme function. In man this movement of chief interest to us has passed forward to its completion. The overshadowing cerebrum crowns, covers, con-

trols all the mesencephalic ganglia ; the hemispheres of thought gather on their inner surface
the innumerable motor and sensor fibres of the
corona by which to rule the physical world, and
open their outer surfaces to the free impulses of
mind, that spiritual power that does its work without betraying its presence, that touches the keys
of action till every fibre pulsates with force, yet
remains itself the same invisible, spiritual agency.

CHAPTER V.

ANIMAL LIFE AS ORGANIC.

WITH the brief sketch now given of the nervous system in its gradations and gradual enlargements before us, we are better able to understand its accumulation of functions, the support higher functions receive from lower ones, and the modifications they impose upon lower ones. The first office of a nervous system is the broader and more rapid diffusion of stimulus with a correspondingly quicker response in action. A single ganglion with its branching nerves obviously accomplishes this simplest purpose, while multiplied ganglia with extended connections, increasing closeness of dependence on each other, and more complete centralization, carry forward this function to its highest form in man. In him many more impulses and much slighter ones, if we regard the whole circle of action, are diffused rapidly through the organism, and, though often suffering arrest in consciousness, issue sooner or later in modified conduct.

The second function of the nervous system, growing out of this its first function, is that of coördination. Speedy and general movements make a more extended harmony of action at once possible and necessary. This office the gray matter of the ganglia in some unsearchable way performs. The impulses which come to these centres are not simply reflected back in a mechanical way through all open connections ; each case is specialized, and fitting partial and concurrent movements made to follow. We cannot, in imagination, present the central ganglia as points of intersection for crossing lines, or as reservoirs at which force is accumulated and thence distributed, but as controlled by a plastic power that in a variable way redirects the stimuli according to the purpose to be subserved by them. The frog from which the brain has been taken will strive for a time to remove an irritation by one limb ; failing of this, he will make the same effort by the limb of the opposite side.

This harmony of effort becomes the more complete and wonderful, as different ganglia, quite removed from each other and with very distinct offices, take part in it; as the whole range of activity, organic, sensational and motor, conscious and unconscious, are involved in it. This coördination passes on in perfection, till consciousness, with its supplementary processes and the widest range of senses and the most diversified muscular activity, and complete organic forces, stand ready, like a waiting engine, to be brought forward by the mind in instant, urgent exertion. Yet this nervous system is not a dead but a living instrument in coördination ; not one functionally complete in itself, but wholly dependent on the life it expresses.

A third function resting on the two now mentioned is that of organic unity. Coördination unites motions in single efforts, makes action for the moment complete and concurrent. Organic unity does much more than this. It unites these actions serially through long periods of time in carrying forward the continuous processes of life. It permanently combines and simultaneously modifies very different functions of organs scattered through the body, subjects them to passing conditions of health and strength, and unites them in one complex process of development. It maintains and expresses inherent tendencies, laws of growth and of inheritance, which are the unwritten constitution of every animal. The nervous system thus ministers to and administers that continuous organic growth by which the individual and the species each become a mobile unit, a fixed yet flowing, a simple yet infinitely complex, power. A single ganglion can do comparatively little in forwarding this organic process, a process that is found in a narrow yet a perfectly plain form in the vegetable. Life in the plant does the same inscrutable work as in the animal. The organic unity is simply carried on by the ministration of the nervous system to more completeness.

The multiplication of ganglia and their connection in one system, combining many forms of muscular effort, as in the varied exertions of attack and

defense ; the addition of special senses by which
the circle of incitements is greatly enlarged ; the
sympathetic dependence of the nutritive and respiratory processes on other activities, concur in the
enlargement of this function of organic unity.
These two forms of coördination, concurrent and
consecutive, the one harmonizing immediate effort,
the other uniting all effort in continuous growth,
arise together, are synchronous directions of one
development, whose primary instrument is the nervous system. A marked step forward is made
when the anterior ganglia overshadow all others,
and we have first an anticipation of cephalization
in the ganglia which gather about the œsophagus,
and later, cephalization itself. The head, with its
numerous ganglia, becomes a visible centre of impressions, and these are combined progressively as
well as diffused laterally through the body. The
greatest step in organic unity is indicated by the
introduction of the cerebellum and cerebrum.
This movement completes itself in the steady enlargement of the cerebrum as the seat of conscious
life, till we have in man a double yet a single coördination, that of the body and that of the mind.
Here are a physical and a mental development
contemporaneous with each other; an involuntary
and unconscious unity, and a voluntary and conscious one which lies above it as the clear heavens
over the earth, and these two, astonishingly separate, yet inseparable, make up the man.

But this leads us to the fourth function of the
nervous system, which, while it rests on previous

ones, especially that of organic unity, greatly enlarges them, and is something more than they, to
wit, conscious life. We must dwell for a little on
this function in its relation to previous ones, for on
a knowledge of this relation must depend the success of our entire discussion. Conscious life
brings increase, modification and a positive increment of its own to lower functions, already well
established and carrying forward by themselves a
very independent and complete work.

Life, as a manifestation, may be divided into
two forms, automatic life and conscious life. They
express the different conditions under which the
vital power acts. The second rests upon and enlarges the first. Automatic life constantly exists
by itself, never conscious life, at least within our
experience. Yet conscious life, when it is added
to automatic life, is a new element, passes more
and more into the ascendency, and ultimately sinks
the automatic life into ministration to itself.

Automatic life has two forms or stages, functional or organic life, adaptive or instinctive life.
The first turns primarily on the interior economy
of the living thing ; the second on its secondary
relations to the environment, its special mastery
over its conditions. Conscious life has also two
stages, associative life and rational life, a life of
experience correlated in memory, and a life of experience correlated in reason. These four forms
of life are by no means separable from each other
with definite bounds, much less as distinct facts.
Each higher one grows out of the lower ones,

modifies them, is modified and sustained by them, disappears insensibly as we pass downward, and arises insensibly as we pass upward. Yet the four forms do not lie on equal terms in the line of development. The first and the last are more permanent than the two intermediate ones.

Organic life starts in the simplest forms, indeed may be said to start without form, without specific functions, as in protoplasm, and in its first manifestation to issue in functions and forms.* All through the vegetable kingdom we have organic life, passing up into increasing complexity. Its great offices are there outlined. Organs are set apart to specific offices, and are united in one complex activity, which ministers to each separately and to all collectively. Thus the plant is truly organized, combines many forces in wonderful energy, puts these by a definite relation to its environment in an external harmony akin with their internal harmony and ministering to it, and passes in descent these complex plastic powers as life from parent to offspring.

Organic life does this work more completely higher up; but does nothing essentially different in kind or more wonderful. It simply makes its material more pliant, multiplies its offices, and so gives successive grades of foundation for later stages of development.

---

* Dr. Foster in his Text-book of Physiology enumerates these six organic properties of simple protoplasm, (1) it is contractile; (2) it is irritable; (3) it is receptive and assimilative; (4) it is metabolic and secretory; (5) it is respiratory; (6) it is reproductive.

Nothing in living things can be understood without this organic power. It is the very pith of the whole procedure, and is akin to what lies below it ; first, to the constructive forces which build the snow-flake, or shape the crystal tree on the window-pane ; secondly, to the forces that lower down act as affinities and attractions, and so give the first elements of order.

The organic life includes the adjustment of organs in office, form, position and in interaction, to each other and to one living product unfolding itself in growth ; and also their momentary adjustment to external conditions, so far as this is directly involved in this evolution. This last adjustment to the conditions of the environment has many gradations, and in its successive phases gives occasion to organic, instinctive, associative and rational life. An organ as an organ may be called on to deal directly with an external element, as leaves with air and light, roots with soil and moisture, the lungs with the atmosphere, and the stomach with food. Or an organ may deal with elements already within the system, and that have been modified by the action of previous organs. Thus the inner layer of the bark is active in growth ; the processes of absorption, filtration and secretion go on in the animal. Or an organ like the heart contributes mechanically to the transfer of material. Here are three grades of dependence on external elements : that of organs which deal directly with external elements ; that of organs that deal with material already modified by previous vital action ; and that of organs which aid in the interior transfer of material. These functions are all strictly organic, imply a plastic power which exactly discriminates qualities and relations, carefully modifies material, skilfully uses it, and performs these offices by distinct organs, working for common ends, both immediate and remote. This first circle of action is the organic circle, and passes by insensible gradations into outer circles of more indirect ministration. These fundamental processes start at the very beginning, in a rudimentary obscure way, and go forward, built up around the same centre, with increasing complexity and completeness, to the very end. Far on in their development, the nervous system becomes their chief instrument in rapid and harmonious action. But they have reached this point none the less through long spaces with no nervous system whatever. In a general way, the direct appropriation, distribution and use of material in growth by the living thing is the office of organic life. On this first combination of functions, there begins early to be induced a second, arising from the fact that food, the material of growth, is not for any kind of life evenly distributed, and hence must be sought after. Plants require their own favoring localities, and have limited means of seeking them and of distribution in them. Though the lower animals are as fixed as plants, mobility rapidly increases as we pass upward, and gives occasion to new and more external forms of activity. With this provision which the animal makes for its own nourishment concurs also the provision in various directions which it is called on to make for its offspring. These secondary adaptations to its circumstances give occasion to the first enlargements of organic life.

We have in the plant discriminating action, by which, within a narrow range, it fits itself to this inequality of conditions. The plumule seeks the air and the light, the radicle the soil and the darkness; the tree in the forest sends out its branches toward the strongest light, and its roots toward the most nutritious areas. There is a certain effort set up in behalf of the best conditions of growth within its narrow field. In various other ways, also, as we have sufficiently shown, in its leaves, tendrils, twining and flowering, it directly adjusts itself to its circumstances, and takes on a secondary activity that favors the organic life.

The offshoots of plants, as stolons, suckers and runners, are vital methods of distribution, by which the young plant receiving a new position secures food. They are a movement by which the parent-plant institutes in its immediate environment what we may figuratively call an active search for a new centre. The same is true of the plant in the distribution of seeds. There are very various and very general means by which seeds, directly or indirectly, are cast into new soil, more or less remote from the parent plant, while this scattering of the seed in search of an open soil is frequently secured by an adjustment of the plant to the mechanical conditions about it, so that the seed may float on the air or on the water to its new locality, or be borne thither by animals. The plant occasionally, as in the Geranium and the Impatiens, sows its seeds directly by its own effort, ordered as an organic power.

The plant may, also, as we have seen, directly capture its food by organic action. The whole process of preparation, decoy and seizure, exhibited in a thousand forms in the animal, is summarized in the plant as an organic function.

The plastic power of the plant maintains, then, all activity within the plant which is necessary to growth. It selects food from the material at hand, assimilates it, distributes it to the points of growth, and builds itself up by it in a living way. In a narrow circle it does more than this. It seeks the stimulating agents, the nutritive conditions, in its immediate surroundings, and by direct appropriation pushes forward its growth. It provides through its progeny for a larger distribution of its life, and a more extended search for food. Again, as a purely organic function, in full anticipation of the most recondite processes of higher life, it forms its seeds and by them transmits its own qualities. The law of descent is here in force, though not with the same fulness as in portions of the animal kingdom. The seeds of plants in some instances transmit with less certainty the secondary characteristics of the parent stalk than do the young of animals. In compensation for this the plant has more variety in its methods of transmission. The twig, though grafted into a new stalk, and fed by alien sap, is faithful in every particular to its own fruit. This is a striking instance of inscrutable organic power, a law of relation, to be interpreted only by that intangible coherence of method which makes life to be life in each department.

This organic life of the plant, though pushing in so many directions, is greatly enlarged in the animal. Starting with processes not to be distinguished from those of the vegetable, it advances by slight increments and with no change of base up to that high form of it we find in the Vertebrata. When the nervous system, which is to become the controlling feature of animal organic life, enters, it does so in a most elementary form. It takes upon itself no new function, but simply facilitates the discharge of old ones. All the way on it holds the same relation to previous processes. It slowly works its way into the plastic power, and becomes to it more and more the primary means of expression. It builds on the organic structure already present, facilitates functions, modifies them, and slowly enlarges them in their application. This steady development of functions, their primary relation to organic life, their later secondary relation to it through the mediation of the nervous system, and their subsequent expansion by the instinctive life, and appropriation by associative and rational life—these are the data of comparative psychology. We shall find it impossible to separate these phases of development from each other, to divide the organic life of the animal from the organic life below it, or from the higher forms of life that in turn spring from it. These phases of growth are not less real and important as marking progress because we cannot separate them each from each, nor indicate exactly the point at which they arise, nor arrange them serially, except in reference to their full manifestations. The actions and reactions are so many and constant in a living thing, that development in one direction necessitates development in other directions; and all development, while springing out of the ground already occupied, proceeds at once to modify and enlarge it. The nervous system, as a new instrument at the disposal of the constructive tendency, takes the relations already established, puts upon them its own new conditions, and so carries forward the organic life into a wonderful complexity of dependencies and exactness of mutual ministrations.

We draw attention in this unfolding of the organic life through a nervous system to the complete, immediate interaction of all its parts. We need to be impressed in detail with this automatic completeness of our organic functions, in order that we may comprehend the part they play in our higher life.

Take the passage of food through the system. It is in the lower forms of animal life selected in kind and quantity by a constitutional impulse or appetite. Brought within the reach of the organic movement, it is automatically swallowed, churned in digestion automatically, passed through the intestines, and so out of the system, by a self-sufficient method. The food itself, by virtue of its very presence, supplies in every stage of progress the exact stimulus to the nervous system needful for the continuation of the process of consumption. Thus, this system mediates between the causes and the effects, and the muscles, acted on by the facts of the case as an immediate positive incitement, carry the work automatically forward to its completion. This nervous stimulus, throughout an unconscious term whose very mode of being is unknown to us, expresses each specific condition, and acts directly on the muscles and other organs involved, to carry forward the process of digestion in its mechanical and its chemical agencies, in its appropriations and in its rejections. Whatever modifications of method arise, there are corresponding modifications of stimuli, and the movement still goes forward in the darkness of purely physical forces. If digestion in the fowl is aided by gravel stones, then it seeks and devours these as certainly as it does food. If the animal ruminates, then it restores the food to the mouth by a movement as mechanical as that by which it swallows it. In connection with this purely organic action, which we may believe proceeds in the lower animals without any consciousness, and in much the larger share of its terms is without consciousness even in man, there are established, as life develops, adjunct processes which may be wholly voluntary or partially so. The securing of food by man, its selection and preparation, are thrown on the judgment and will, while its mastication, as a condition of farther discrimination and of pleasure, mingles the voluntary with the involuntary, the latter predominating. In the higher animals there is the same union of the two concurrent elements, the automatic gaining ground at every step downward. The unconscious life is thus the basis of the conscious life in three respects. Life is, first, far advanced by a purely automatic action ; second, it at length leaves secondary, outlying offices to be taken up by voluntary effort ; and, third, the automatic process remains to the very end the substance of that organic system to which the conscious action ministers, and on which it is perpétually expended. Very little consciousness in man attends digestion after the food has passed through mastication, and that which does attend it has little or nothing to do with the continuation of the action. The integrity of this automatic movement in man is seen in sickness. The patient, when quite unconscious, may swallow, if the food is introduced into the mouth. In perfect health we find ourselves unable frequently to check the involuntary movement after it has once laid hold of the food, passed to the rear of the mouth.

The circulation of the blood offers another example. This, through the muscles of the heart and the muscular linings of the arteries, is largely the result of mechanical force. This force is applied rhythmically and harmoniously in all parts of the body, by virtue of the intervention of the nervous system, automatically associating all the states and actions involved with each other as causes and effects. The circulation of the blood, laden with

food or with waste, is thus gently and continuously
carried forward through the entire body, with
momentary reference to the specific condition of
each member as one of rest or of action.   Activity
or injury in any one part brings with it, through a
change of stimulus, a more full and rapid circulation.   The immediateness of this control of the
blood vessels is seen in blushing, in the sudden
heat which accompanies a blunder in public, and in
the fact that when certain nerves are injured, the
circulation in portions of the body becomes de-
ranged and excessive.   This circulatory system remains, when the conscious life arises, almost wholly
beyond its direct control.   In some instances, however, the will may even reach the beating of the
heart; and states of mind and feeling that are themselves partially voluntary, greatly modify the circulation.   Diffidence, anxiety, fear, courage, patience, are all operative on this branch of life.

A third example of organic mechanism is that
of breathing.   The muscles that control the lungs
must themselves be guided by the immediate condition of the lungs. The nervous system mediates
between the two, receives from each fluctuation appropriate incentives and transfers them to the
muscles involved.   Breathing is not thus a merely
mechanical movement of equal, irresistible, untir-
ing strokes; it is flexible every instant, and variable
under a thousand forces.   It is held by the vital
power as the engine by the engineer, when he is
ready to accelerate, retard, arrest or reverse the
motion.   In most animal life this movement is en-

tirely automatic.   In man it is closely united with
the voluntary power, and freely reached by it.
The use of the voice, almost wholly a means with
him of intellectual and emotional expression, requires this superior control of the lungs; so do
many other services, as the employment of a blow-
pipe, or of a wind instrument of music, or the holding of the breath in the presence of noxious gases.
The lungs, therefore, with man have an extended
voluntary action induced upon their purely automatic
use, and sustained in turn by it.   Thus throughout
the animal organism, every movement, every action,
muscular and glandular, is harmonized by inscrutable nervous stimuli, which the present facts call
out in the nerves, and which these pass over to
muscles and organs as controlling force.   Nor is
this wonderful response to changing conditions confined to single lines of action, like digestion and
respiration, but covers completely their relations to
each other and to the immediate and remote wants
of the organism.   If digestion is active, other movements tend to moderation ; but if muscular effort
is increased, the circulation is increased and the
breathing made more rapid and full.   If the brain
is busy, the flow of blood is directed toward it, and
digestion is slackened.   Moments of rest, on the
other hand, accrue at once to the benefit of nutri-
tion, and thus prepare the way for the next putting
forth of power.   Even the intangible feelings send
waves of modification over this interlaced mechanism.   Embarrassment forces the blood to the face
and fear drives it out ; alarm makes the heart throb,

and courage sends the life-currents briskly forward
to every limb.   There are various examples of passing sensations which are instantly responded to by
decided muscular or glandular action.   An irritation in the nostrils produces sneezing, in the throat
coughing, in the eye tears, in the side laughter.
One condition of the nerves issues in stretching,
another in cramps, and another in spasms.   How
subtile are those impressions, half physical, half intellectual, which automatically carry a yawn from
person to person in a company or in an audience !
This last fact especially deserves our attention.   An
organic system which can receive and express unconsciously such obscure, transient and sympathetic impulses, shows that the range of automatic
action in it is still very great, notwithstanding so
much of the field has been covered by voluntary
life.

But these pervasive and changing stimuli of
every terminus of the sensory nerves are farther supplemented by nerves specialized in position and
function to the discernment of certain external conditions.   These are the special senses.   The nerves
terminating in the external tissues of the body from
the beginning, without doubt, turned conditions of
contact into stimuli, as merely organic matter had
been able in a less degree to do before them.   Nor
need we suppose this power limited to mechanical
contact alone.   Heat and light may well enough
act directly on a general nervous organization,
since they act even on plants.   Odor and taste, not
in their final conscious forms, but as disturbing

chemical conditions, may readily pass into organic stimuli. Sound as vibration may easily give a nervous impulse, the instant any part of the animal is nicely poised enough to respond in movement to it. Hearing is quite another thing. If we make touch in some form the parent of the senses, we are not to imagine that touch, as the conscious sense it now is in man, stands on terms of close agreement with other primitive susceptibilities, any more than our vision is the vision of the star-fish. Touch itself has had its development. In some parts of the body it exhibits its full power as a special sense, in other portions it gives rise to a disagreeable tickling, in others it occasions convulsive laughter, while in most parts it yields only a vague sense of contact. Nor are we for a moment to forget that the conscious experiences which accompany our special senses are additional to this automatic action, and that this proceeds quite independently of these intellectual terms. It is not by volition through consciousness that we twitch away the irritated limb, or laugh when we are tickled. The action may follow quite against our will, and we give signs of pleasure when we are thoroughly angry. The interior and exterior stimuli struggle with each other, and sometimes anger vanquishes laughter, and sometimes laughter anger.

Consciousness may not accompany, and probably does not accompany, the action of the special senses, till they are comparatively complete in their development, and extended in their range ; they are then ready to furnish the conditions of experience, and to be aided in their government of the body by the coördination of consciousness. Prior to this, consciousness would be an expenditure of energy to no purpose.

This automatic action is apparent from the very rudimentary form in which the organs of special senses first offer themselves. The incipient eye consists of a " colored spot," obviously incapable of any other discrimination than a very obscure one between light and darkness. "Among the lower Articulata the development of the visual apparatus does not seem to pass this rudimentary grade."* It is only slowly that the eye acquires a range by which it reveals distant objects. The eye of the snail, on its extended peduncle, seems to do little more than to enable it slightly to anticipate contact, and to increase the sensitiveness of the organ as a feeler. A darkness and a light that can be *felt* are the earliest conditions of vision.

Hearing is developed even more tardily and obscurely than sight. It is supposed to be present as an incipient stimulus even when no organ is discoverable. All that is essential to hearing is a nerve so located and covered that it can respond to the vibrations of the air. In most kinds of Medusae, there are found along the margin of the disk peculiar sacculi, containing bodies which easily receive a vibratory movement. This construction remains in the Mollusca the model of the organ of hearing, and a sack with its otoliths opens the nervous system to the impressions of sound. This sense

* Carpenter's Comparative Physiology, p. 726.

is slowly developed in this direction of organic conditions that give a more and more complete response to the vibrations of the air. There is nothing to indicate the transition line beyond which the physical stimulus begins to pass up into consciousness as sound, but the simplicity of its early action indicates its automatic character, and in all its later complexity and habitual ministration to the thoughts, we find still that a remnant of its direct and purely organic effect remains to it. Its results in consciousness when they enter are additional to its physical effects, and while they serve later to recombine and so greatly to modify these first results, the organic force of sound remains none the less throughout the basis of much automatic action in this sense. The physical movement sustains the mental one no matter to what degree it is modified by it, and the highest sense may resume in a portion of its action the simplicity and directness of a physical stimulus.

A second proof that the special senses were not from the beginning attended by consciousness, is found in their nervous connections and offices. The question whether the early action of the senses did or did not involve consciousness is one of moment, as it helps us to understand the extent and value of the purely organic element in our constitution. The number of eyes, or ocelli, for they fall much short of what we ordinarily mean by an eye, show them to be merely points of narrow, local excitement. In the oyster and other headless Mollusca, distinct ocelli are distributed over both margins of

the mantle.   They vary in number from forty to two
hundred ; and the oyster closes its shell when a
shadow falls on these pigment spots.* These ocelli,
thus, by their number, position and office indicate
that they are the medium of an automatic impulse.
In the razor-fish, the cockle, and other bivalves possessing siphon-tubes, the eyes are situated either
at the base or on the tips of the numerous small
tentacles distributed around the orifices of these
tubes, which, in those living in the sand, are often
the only parts appearing above the surface.† Their
evident purpose to distinguish the light of the surface leaves little doubt that their action is automatic.
The star-fish is furnished with these eye-spots at
the tip of each ray, and they are united to the central ganglion of the ray.   Their direct government
is evidently confined to a single arm, and only indirectly reaches other portions of the body.   In the
Mollusca they are sometimes connected with the
posterior and sometimes with the anterior ganglia.
In the headless Mollusca the senses of touch and
of sight are chiefly developed in dependence on the
posterior ganglia.   The auditory saccules also stand
in connection with the pedal ganglia, evincing an
immediate government of the motion of the animals.   Prof. Bastian, in the article just referred to,
says : "In these headless mollusks, therefore, the
functions pertaining to the brain in other animals
are distributed in a very remarkable manner, and the
anterior ganglia can not in them be regarded as

* Popular Science Monthly, vol. ix. p. 218.
† Ibid. vol. x. p. 30.

representing such an organ."*   "In certain Annel-
lida," says Dr. Carpenter, "it is singular that eyes exactly resembling those elsewhere found in the *head*
should present themselves in the extremity of the
tail, whose movement they obviously seem to direct."†

We infer then the unconscious character of the
special senses in their origin and early development
from their very rudimentary character, from their
very restricted range as indicated by their number,
form their direct connection with scattered ganglia
of motion, and from the want of any superior centre at which conscious states could be united and
harmonized in motion.

If it be urged that consciousness may accompany
this automatic action without controlling it, we answer that consciousness itself involves an expenditure of force, and if the organic circuit is complete
without it, a superfluous expenditure.   Hence natural selection would work against this purely wasteful
element and eliminate it.   If consciousness is an
inoperative force in the lower action of the special
senses, we have no right to presume it to be present.
This is the more obvious when we remember how
often and how readily the higher senses, even in
man who uses them primarily as the instruments
of his voluntary life, drop into purely automatic
connections.

Other facts looking to the same conclusion, the
tardy development of consciousness, are found in

---

* Popular Science Monthly, vol. x. p. 31.
† Comparative Physiology, p. 726.

vivisection, in diseases of the cerebrum, and in the deficiencies or even entire absence of this organ. We can hardly doubt that the cerebrum is, in the Vertebrata, the exclusive seat of consciousness. Theory and experiment confirm this conclusion. But if the cerebrum is removed, there is a large remainder in various animals of automatic action, a remainder that varies in completeness according to the extent in them of voluntary action. This strictly organic action includes all the senses, and extends even to cries of pain. These, when purely reflex, are distinguishable from similar cries which accompany consciousness, and no more indicate pain than do the groans of a patient while under the influence of an anæsthetic. Thus the organic life is controlled by blind stimuli, when the conditions of consciousness are seen to be wanting. This automatic action we may well believe would be more complete, when united in the higher animals to the usual condition of intelligence, than when left mutilated and fragmentary by a violent stripping away of its adjuncts. The conscious life, in shaping the organic life, must constantly tend to put upon it limitations, which would appear very manifest when the intertwined conscious element is violently removed. It is remarkable that so large a portion of the organic action still remains unimpaired, when dealt with so suddenly and severely in vivisection.

In the same way disease may greatly reduce conscious action in man or quite subvert it, and still there may remain automatic action extending even to the highest senses. Infants have been born without any cerebrum, and the organic life has held fast for a time to its own narrow basis. In extreme idiocy, the circle of consciousness may be narrowed down to a very uninfluential term, yet the senses be complete. On the other hand, as in a Laura Bridgman, the circle of the senses may be greatly diminished, and the powers of a conscious life, when once awakened, be found unusually vigorous.

Another consideration, showing the long priority of the purely organic life, is the large part it still plays, even in connection with the highest intelligence. It is the dark region in which the powers of mind hide all their roots. The eye is the most voluntary sense, yet it is momentarily sustained by purely automatic, physical action. The iris contracts and expands with the light. The muscles of the eyes mechanically adjust themselves to the objects to be seen, lengthening or shortening the axis of each eye, and separating or converging the axes of the two, as the distances require. To this are added the movements of the eyes with every change of position in the object seen, or in the person beholding it, or with every change occasioned by their conjoint movement. How rapid, complicated and still complete these adjustments may become, is seen in a game of ball. There is a kind of physical inspiration in a skilful blow of the bat. The winking of the eyes, and their closing under strong light, are of the same direct character. The way in which vision unconsciously attends on our action is made plain by the difficulties we meet with in stumbling along an uneven snow-path in the night-time.

In many animals there are spontaneous movements of the ears, allied to those of the eyes. The slightest motions of the air instantly set at work this automatic mechanism by which sound is gathered. In man a sudden noise startles the muscular system, and puts it in an attitude of apprehensive readiness. This immediate effect of sounds may go much farther, as in the hunter, who is made habitually observant of them, or in the musician in the orchestra, who more or less mechanically suits his action to the action of those about him.

In sleep slight irritations are responded to, and the sleeper repeatedly readjusts himself so as to relieve fatigue and secure comfort. In somnambulism this apparently unconscious response to external conditions is carried very far, so far as to enable the sleep-walker to do things which would be difficult or impossible for him in waking hours.

Skill, as in the acquisition of a trade, turns on this mingled dependence and independence of the organic life, and consists in the passage of voluntary into automatic movement. Connections at first conscious, partial and laborious, become unconscious, complete and spontaneous ; automatic action takes the new direction, and the man has acquired skill, he has planted new dependencies in his physical constitution. How complicated these dependencies are, and in how many different degrees they remain under the influence of the conscious life, are seen in ordinary and extraordinary activities. In walking any inequality of the ground is provided for by an automatic modification of the muscles through the eye, so much so that a mistake to the extent of an inch brings a concussion. In reading, however rapidly, every letter affects the articulation, and, this too, when we are paying no attention either to the process or to the subject-matter. Page after page can be passed over in moments of abstraction without a slip, though many thousand adjustments of the organs of speech are involved. When a mistake does occur, it often enters in a mechanical way. The first letter of one word may be brought back and made to introduce another word, while the letter that it displaces is carried forward to fill the vacancy. Thus in type, the opening syllables of adjacent lines are transferred. The mingling of the involuntary and the voluntary in the playing of a superior musician is very wonderful.

Training may be attached to different senses and to different series of sensations. An action which is accompanied by this indirect oversight of the eye can hardly be performed without it, though we are not ordinarily conscious of the aid rendered. One writes without seeming to guide the pen, and while busily occupied with the topic ; yet, if the eye is diverted, the movement becomes at once irregular and vague. One is quite certain to strike his fingers in driving a nail, if the light is inadequate, though he may know the precise posi-

tion of the nail, and ordinarily drives it without
hesitation.   Yet practice may enable us to do
these and like acts under the unconscious guidance
and correction of touch.   In one remarkable instance, given by Dr. Carpenter, a mother was
unable to govern the muscles of the arm by the
ordinary automatic connections, and would unconsciously drop her child unless she watched the
movements of her arms, and guided them by the
eye.   She held her infant safely so long as she
looked at it, but lost it when her attention was
turned away.

Sleights of hand and feats . of equilibrists give
these acquired yet automatic connections in a
striking form.   A second unusual activity has by
patient effort and a pliant organic system been engrafted on the common one, and become with it an
available constituent. .

In the training which is to issue in this increase
of organic action, this enlarged correlation of nervous stimuli, the voluntary purpose works in a very
obscure way.   We can not at all trace in consciousness the lines of connections established between our nerves and muscles in the fulfilment of
our purposes.   We send into the automatic mechanism a blind, tentative impulse, and it comes forth
a harmonious and graceful action; if the movement is less successful, we repeat it till it completes itself in perfect coördination.   We are not
more aware of the hidden dependencies by which
our will is accomplished, than a stranger, shifting
a band in complicated machinery, is aware of the

connections which suddenly modify its action. I
roll my head and still direct my eyes to one object.
I utter a difficult word, I make a somersault; in
each case I propose to do the act, and do it, but
may have no knowledge of the means by which it
is done, nor can I follow in consciousness one of
the fugitive stimuli that are flashing through my
system. I have within my own body a veritable
power of conjuration. The conscious purpose falls
as a mystic utterance on the purely organic powers, and these hasten to fulfil its command. We
are constantly overlooking this fact, and so ascribe
much more to intelligence and much less to the
inherent, self-sufficing tendencies, than belong to
them.

We see then (1) that the unconscious organic
connections are long prior to the conscious ones,
and their sole basis; (2) that conscious activity,
when it comes, avails itself of and increasingly
modifies the organic connections; (3) that the unconscious activities, while they thus secure a larger
range, remain the same in essential nature; (4)
that the superior power finds more explanation in
the lower one than the lower one in the higher
one; (5) that in every stage of development there
must be relative completeness in the organic element, and that the conscious element slowly builds
upon it, as physically secondary to it, though intellectually primary. Consciousness is always sinking in the development of intelligence deeper and
deeper into the organic mechanism. It follows
from this (6) that the same organic connections

are, in the lower forms of life, more absolutely
complete in themselves than in the higher forms
of life.   In our earlier interpretations we are to lay
stress on the predominant organic element : all
presumptions are in its favor.   We are to refer
nothing to intelligence till intelligence has manifestly been established as a modifying power.   (7)
Increments are decisive, and are enlarged downward ; they are not evolved upward.   It is intelligence that comes as a new factor to organize structure, and modifies and partially displaces even its
prior action ; it is not this prior action that slowly
divulges itself as intelligence.

When, therefore, we interpret low organizations
by ourselves, and speak of sea-anemones as without
doubt manifesting will, we are simply giving play
to fancy, or quite misapprehending the whole constructive development of animal life.*

While this organic mechanism, ever amplifying
and varying its functions within its own limits, remains throughout the core of growth, it needs to
be supplemented by activities more external, more
changeable, by which it may be put in larger connection with its environment.   This is accomplished, first, by the muscular system as controlled
by special instincts and special senses, later by the
associations of experience, and last by rational activity.   We have, therefore, in order, these three
additive developments, separated by vanishing lines,
to consider, instinctive, associative, and rational
life.

* Popular Science Monthly, vol. vii. p. 8.

CHAPTER VI.

ANIMAL LIFE AS INSTINCTIVE.

INSTINCTS in the growth of intelligence lie between the grades occupied by strictly organic life and by intelligence proper. It is not strange that the organic life, which primarily sustains in their many complicated and changeable relations the internal organs and functions of the living thing, and secondarily, though in a way inseparable from its first office, controls the actions of the animal towards its environment, should, in this large open direction, extend itself in increasingly subtile and varied adjustments. It is no more wonderful that external action should be capable of extensive control by the organic stimuli of an automatic nervous system, everywhere reaching the surface, and appearing in many points as special senses, than it is that such a system should take cognizance of the slightest internal changes, and fit to them the accompanying muscular action. The same sensitiveness directed toward external changes which we find in operation in internal changes, would give a very complete scheme of conduct.

This is what takes place in instinct. The organic life, by virtue of obscure stimuli received in the nervous system, automatically controls many actions which relate to surrounding conditions, to the present and future wants of the animal or of its posterity, and so gives an appearance of intelligence which is not present.

Nor is it strange when intelligence in its higher forms arrives, as in man, that it should take possession of most of this field, previously occupied in lower lives with instincts. This shifting of the dividing line in different grades of life between organic action and intelligence, if it is not clearly recognized, leads to much confusion. It is in perfect keeping with what we find everywhere. There are no firm bounds between the grades of life, but flexible ones, swayed now to this side, now to the other. It is in accordance with analogy that organic action should pass into associative and rational action, by an area of obscure and mixed phenomena, having different attachments, backward or forward, at different times. It is natural that the lower, once taken up into the higher, should be greatly modified by it ; that the higher should penetrate into and occupy territory in whole or in part which had previously fallen to the lower, pushing back inferior processes before its own superior ones, and weaving the two together at a new line of junction. Indeed, if the organic life kept strictly within its inner circle of organic functions, the transition to intelligence would be abrupt, and with no sufficient preparation or support. The feeble germs of conscious life must be nursed into power by extended and well-sustained automatic action, or they would perish from the excess of work thrown upon them, from their inability to assume the guidance of the life from which they were just budding forth.

It seems equally plain, also, that when intelligence becomes a vigorous, pushing power, lower forms must retreat before it and mould themselves afresh to it; otherwise the animal would lose its unity, and remain inflexible and resistful under the new authority. The new centre must send new radii into the old field, or it remains a comparatively separate and dead addition. There must be living territory over which the new life can spread itself.

We look, then, upon instincts as occupying this intermediate field over which the organic forces first slowly extend in an automatic adaptation of the various forms of life to their environment, and from which, in the higher animals and in man, they again slowly retreat, partially or entirely, as intelligence comes forward to supersede them.

That there are instincts, and that collectively they cover a very extended domain, cannot be doubted. This has been the view that philosophy, science, and common conviction have spontaneously taken up. Recently some efforts have been made greatly to narrow, or wholly to remove this division, and to refer to instruction and conscious adaptation what had been previously ascribed to instinct. This effort has drawn out careful experiments that have served fully to confirm the general impression, and to establish instinctive action.

The most noteworthy of these observations have been made by D. A. Spalding. The results have

appeared in various scientific publications, have occupied attention for a considerable period, and
have become familiar to all interested in these questions.   These observations and experiments were
made on the young of domestic animals, chickens,
turkeys, ducks and pigs.   It was found that these
young animals respond at once and decisively to
external conditions of sight and sound quite independently of experience ; that they go to work in a
complete, masterly way in handling themselves, in
suiting action to existing facts, in taking and cap-
turing food, or in meeting danger.   The theory of
instruction and rapid acquisition is quite ruled out.
We are, therefore, at liberty to assume instincts as a
fact, and also the extended and important part
which they play in animal life.   We should define
instinct to be the automatic tendency which underlies an organic action having the form of an intelligent and voluntary one.   The impulse rests in the
organic life, the form of the action allies it to intelligence.   Instincts will, therefore, disappear below in stated, organic activities, and pass above
into intelligent conduct.   The field is preëminently
mixed, one of overlapping and diverse, though in
each single case of concurrent, activities.   This
definition makes instinct cover the same ground as
that assigned to it by Mr. Lewes.   He says that
"instinct is lapsed intelligence."   The definition is
to be objected to, not on the ground that it does
not point in the right direction for the facts, but
because it implies a theory as to the origin and relation of the facts, and that, too, an incorrect one.

Instincts are to be regarded as the action of lower forces in unusual vigor, rather than as the sinking of higher forces in relative decay. To this point we shall return.

A definition of instinct is not so important as it would be, if the field of this form of action possessed any well-defined margin. Our definition suffices to direct attention to the right phenomena, to give their leading characteristics, and to cover the facts that are discussed under this head by the great majority of scientific writers. The word, *instinct*, is greatly extended by some, so as to include the habits and even the intuitions of rational life. This extension confounds very different things on the ground of a superficial resemblance. Instinct belongs exclusively to physical action, and its chief interest pertains to the nature and the origin of the impulses which underlie it. It is difficult to speak of the one without involving the other ; to define the nature of instinct without at least implying a theory of its origin. Kirby and Spence, while declining a definition, say. "We may call the instincts of animals those unknown faculties implanted in their constitution by the Creator, by which, independent of instruction, observation or experience, and without a knowledge of the end in view, they are impelled to the performance of actions tending to the well-being of the individual and the preservation of the species."*
Says Darwin, " An action, which we ourselves require experience to enable us to perform, when per-

* Entomology, p. 537.

formed by an animal, more especially by a very young one, without experience, and when performed by many individuals in the same way, without their knowing for what purpose it is performed, is usually said to be instinctive."* Our definition or description of instincts takes in, then, the two elements which characterize these actions, a constitutional tendency expressing itself in work which has the form of intelligent activity.

We proceed to a more careful consideration of the nature and origin of these midway facts which help to bridge the space between automatic and voluntary, unconscious and conscious, activity. Instinctive actions have the appearance of being directed by intelligence. Any movement obviously organic, like the pulsation of the lungs or of blood-vessels, would not be referred to instinct, no matter how complicated the dependencies. But why are actions which appear to imply on the part of the animal a perception of ends and an adaptation of means to them separated from intelligence, put in a class by themselves, and referred to instinct? Notwithstanding a decided tendency to narrow down the circle of instinct, there remain actions known as instinctive, which we cannot refer to intelligence. There are a certainty and precision in them, and a uniformity in method and results, which obviously distinguish them from actions which are the results of variable foresight and choice. Intelligence does not present in its methods the exact, and comparatively unchanging phases which so

* Origin of Species, p. 205.

plainly belong to instinct. Existing in every variety
of degree, and acting under very changeable circumstances, intelligence is correspondingly capricious in its results. Whatever uniformity there is
in them in successive generations is chiefly to be
ascribed to imitation and instruction. But imitation and instruction are out of the question in pro-
nounced instincts. Such a transfer is the supposition which observation and experiment have settled
in the negative. The superficial form, then, of the
instinctive action, though resembling in some relations the products of intelligence, is after all quite
unlike them; while its transmission attends on the
organic and not the imitative powers.

Moreover, the animal whose habits of life are instinctive does not show that development, nor present, beyond its own range of activity, that adaptation of means to ends, which we should have a right
to expect from it, if its daily conduct were the result of thought. The bee and the ant are remarkable workers within a somewhat broad range of life,
but the boundaries of their knowledge are comparatively unchangeable. Intelligence must always present vanishing lines, and pass from mastery to weakness along many obscure paths. The bee builds its
comb in a wonderful way, but builds little else that
is wonderful. It neither climbs up to the maximum
structure by gradations, nor finds elsewhere kindred
fields for the application of its principles. This sol-
itariness and disassociation of its best work must
strike at once the most careless observer. The ant,
though an adept in arched and tunneled work, can

not be induced to frame the simplest bridge to meet
an unusual exigency.   Sir John Lubbock describes
his efforts to draw out in them a temporary device.
He left a chasm in a paper bridge so wide that the
ants could not quite reach across it.   " They came
to the edge and tried hard to get over, but it did not
occur to them to push the paper bridge, though the
distance was only about one-third of an inch, and
they might easily have done so.   *   *   *
Thinking that the paper was a substance to which
they were not accustomed, I tried the same with a
bit of straw one inch long and one-eighth of an inch
wide.   The result was the same."*   He strove to
induce them to build a bridge of mould ; to drop the
food they were carrying, or themselves to drop, a
short distance and to save a long journey ; " but
these simple expedients did not occur to them,"
though they obviously desired to overcome the difficulty.   The narrowness of their devices in one
direction thus stands in striking contrast with their
breadth in other directions.

It is also to be remembered that if instinctive
action is to be referred to reason, it must often be
reason of a very high order.   Though the comb of
the bee has not all the perfection sometimes ascribed
to it, it is still a very exact and very extraordinary
structure, and, as wholly the product of thought,
would imply very extraordinary powers, even if we
allow it a slow serial development.   Many instinctive actions, especially those of insects, as the sand-
wasp, have reference to offspring which the parent

* Popular Science Monthly, vol. ii. p. 46.

is never to see, of which it could gain little or no knowledge from experience, nor have toward it any of the ordinary solicitude of natural affection. These instinctive efforts are also made when they are necessarily abortive, or when there is no occasion for them. Thus the hen will sit without eggs, and the bee " store up honey in the hottest climates."*

Very high instincts are also associated with very low intelligence. Certain larvæ, whose nervous development is so elementary as to give very little basis for intelligence, exhibit striking instincts, hardly less so than those of mature insects. The way in which the larva and the insect both prepare the way for each other, though separated by the egg and the chrysalis, and the vigorous instincts of each lying in one line of development, make out a strong case against intelligence. The organic development and the accompanying instincts, must, in each circle of life, have arisen together, as they supplement each other. Moreover, the explanation that is forced upon us in one direction should have its due extension in other directions. If, when the mason-wasp stings the caterpillar which it deposits with its egg in such a manner as to paralyze it without killing it, we refer the action to instinct, we may also refer to instinct the action of the ant in gnawing off the radicle of the grain it stores, that it may not sprout. In the one example the provision is beyond the experience of the insect, in the other example, within it; but in both the methods

* Kirby and Spence's Entomology, p. 537.

and objects are so alike that we naturally refer them to one cause.

There is, however, a far more decisive consideration which for us at once settles the fact of instincts, and gives us their explanation. Many instincts, I think I may say much the majority of them, and the most remarkable of them, are closely associated with peculiar physical powers to which they stand in the relation of functions ; or are incident to the fulfilment of functions. The bee can manufacture by an organic process its wax. Without this power its constructive talent could not exist, and without its constructive talent this organic function would fail of its office. It is reasonable, therefore, to suppose that a peculiar constitutional power of this sort should carry organically with it, like every other portion of the body, the automatic connections necessary for its one normal manifestation. The organ and the function correlate, and find their simple expression in the instinctive action. So the silk-worm and a thousand other worms could not construct their cocoons, if they could not spin the filaments of which they are made. The hornet must be able to fabricate his paper home ; the cliff-swallow to cement the material of its nest ; the chimney-swallow to glue together the twigs that sustain its eggs ; the working ant to temper its mortar ; the fighting ant to secrete its poisonous acid ; the beetle to generate the disagreeable odor by which it defends itself ; and the wasp to sting the deposited caterpillar. The wonderful and varied devices of the spider are correlative to its spinneret, and thus a large class of instincts, than which none are more remarkable, is dependent on a very peculiar physical organ.

We are also to remember that many instincts are associated with the propagation of the species, and so may find an immediate organic impulse in the susceptible procreative organs. Beetles and insects generally show very clear and decisive instincts in the depositing of their eggs, and in the provision for offspring. Many of the most remarkable adaptations of means to ends in this class of animals arise at this point. The migrations and nesting of birds, and the burrows and retreats of higher animals, are more or less directly associated with this strong and pervasive organic tendency. Another example of instinctive actions united to very peculiar organic powers, is offered by the chameleon and the squid. The ability which this cuttle-fish possesses of removing its spots, and so making itself less conspicuous, must be the basis of that instinctive action by which it in this way conceals its approach from its prey. Nor can we readily believe that working bees understand those very unusual organic changes by which a working grub is transformed by a peculiar diet into a queen ; and that they stand ready, on an exigency, to avail themselves of them. The external conditions, like the internal transformation, seem to be locked up together as parts of one remarkable organic tendency ; nor is it easy to understand how the two could have arisen otherwise than together as parts of the same organic development.

We believe, then, that there is a direct or indirect organic basis for every instinctive action. This supposition, not in itself improbable, seems sufficiently confirmed when we reflect, (*a*) on the extreme subtilty of the stimuli in ordinary organic connections. We can give no explanation of the incitements which coördinate functional actions, nor any term in consciousness which expresses them. Some of these are very peculiar, as the impulse which leads a hen to eat egg-shells ; some arise on very slight occasions, as the stimuli which direct a curlew in unearthing a grub, buried eight or nine inches in the sand, reaching it with a single thrust of the bill, or guides the wood-pecker to his prey ; some exist when the occasions for them seem to have passed away, as the irritations which lead the rattlesnake to strike with the headless body many hours after decapitation.* The obscurity of the connection, therefore, between the organs involved and their modes of activity is not different from that we meet with constantly in animal life. (*b*) There are often, as in the examples already given, and in many more which might be given, special physical powers directly associated with the instinct, and finding their expression in it. The relation between them is so fixed and functional, that a development which should bring the organ without including its instinctive use would be quite futile. (*c*) There is an extensive, complex and varied system, that of reproduction, furnishing the most universal, forcible

* Popular Science Monthly, vol. iv. p. 265.

and subtile organic stimuli, which is closely associated with a large class of instincts. Even in man
this system comes accompanied with the powerful
natural affections. (*a*) The appetites and the special
senses, combined in man in so many automatic ways
by the conscious life, are capable in the animal of a
corresponding extension in unconscious correlations.
The conscious element which accompanies a sensation or an appetite serves indeed to bring it under
the cognition, and so the guidance, of the mind, but
does not necessarily form any part of its physical
power.

To these considerations we add another less
easily appreciated, but one as weighty in itself as
any of them ; (*e*) the peculiar conditions of in
stinctive development in insects. Insects, and
among them preëminently spiders, bees and ants,
offer examples of the highest forms of instinctive
life. What is the reason of this? A point already
urged, that of special organs, applies decisively to
the spider, somewhat less so to the bee, and still less
so to the ant. In the case of the bee and the ant,
which may well enough be put at the head of instinctive life, we need, if possible, further explanation. That the wonderful social development of
these insects is mainly instinctive seems to us plain.
Perfect as may be their organization and methods
of life in any given case, they yet have in the several species the narrowness and rigidity of instinct.
Says Spence: "There is no authentic instance on
record of the hive-bees altering in any age or climate their peculiar operations which are now in the

coldest and in the hottest regions precisely what they were in Greece in the time of Aristotle and in Italy in the days of Virgil." * Having spoken of special adaptations, as the bending of the comb, in order to avoid attaching it to an unsafe surface, like that of glass, he adds, " These variations, however singular, are limited in their extent ; all bees are and have always been able to avail themselves of a certain number, but not to increase that number." † If we compare bees and ants with birds, we shall find the latter more free and variable in their constructive methods, not because they show more skill than the insects, but because a larger share of intelligence and a smaller share of instinct go into their composition. If the habits of the bee and ant are to be referred to reflection, they would appear to be far more thoughtful than birds, and ought to show much more flexibility in their devices.

A portion, also, of their action, if referable to insight, greatly transcends human intelligence. In the construction of domes and arches, bridges, tunnels and covered ways, the ants outstripped man by innumerable ages, and if reflection underlies these structures of theirs, they greatly surpass him now in the relative magnitude and importance of their works.

We shall admit this when we see men build cities or arch over mighty phalansteries without tools, putting the clay into form with naked hands and tempering it with the glue of their mouths.

* Ibid. p. 537. † Ibid. p. 550.

Till something like a parity of methods shall be found between men and ants, we shall believe in the fundamental diversity of the intellectual states from which their respective actions proceed. Agreements which overlook such radical disagreements as these are superficial. What a wonderful comprehension of causes would that be which should induce a change of food for larvæ by the working bees for the purpose of supplying queens! Here is a prescience quite beyond our own, for we are unwilling to believe the facts when they are before us, and have no explanation to offer of them.

But the manner in which these communities are organized and their entire procedure are decisive against intelligence as the controlling force. Thought must, according to its degrees of perfection, have the means of expression. Though thought is not identical with language, and in order of causation precedes it, neither can be developed to any extent without the other. Thought can no more unfold and consolidate its conclusions in the individual mind without its own instrument of expression and retention than it can in the community between man and man. Conjoint, intelligent action, therefore, implies constant and clear intercourse in language, since only by this means can labor be organized and harmonized on an intellectual basis. What could a thousand men accomplish in a common undertaking without language. The popular notion, therefore, and that of patient observers even, has been that bees and ants communicate freely with each other. When Sir J.

Lubbock, in a series of careful experiments cast doubt on this conclusion, there was much unwillingness to accept his results. He seems, however, clearly to have shown that bees and ants communicate but little with each other, far less than has been supposed. It is well-nigh certain that they, like other animals, only impart their own concrete states. The bee is a sensible fact to every other bee ; and its states of quiet and disturbance are a portion of that fact ; as much so as the crossness of a dog to a child, or a smiling face to an infant. Fear and alarm thus spread through a hive as anger through a mob. In this interchange of states the antennæ are serviceable, as are tongues and horns with cows. There is no proof that a bee or an ant ever possesses an abstract truth, or ever imparts one to a companion ; and if they do not, this settles the fact that their combinations in social undertakings are not thoughtful ones. Sir John Lubbock found that if the store of food to be removed was large, the ants who discovered it soon brought companions to aid in the labor. He was also convinced that they do not report directions and plans, that they have but a very limited knowledge of them, and move chiefly by scent.* It is easy to understand how a large supply of food should produce a concrete state of satisfaction in an ant, that could immediately interest its companions and secure their aid. The senses which are most alert in these insects lead to the same conclu-

* Popular Science Monthly, vol. xi. p. 56.

sion. They are inattentive to sounds, guide themselves but little by vision, and have very acute
scent and touch. These are the senses which favor
organic development ; while vision, and above all
hearing, minister to reflection. The frequent in-
sensibility of insects to the disasters of their companions, or to their death, leads us to believe that
relations and duties not instinctively enforced on
them have not much interest for them. Parasites
on bees that could be easily removed by companions are allowed to remain, the sufferer receiving
no aid.

We are also to remember that from a scientific
point of view the social economy of the hive and the
ant-hill takes a very misleading garniture from the
language which the enthusiastic observer applies
to them. He talks of the queen-bee, yet the queen-
bee is not the ruler, but the fecund mother of the
hive, that is all. Her close confinement, her daily
food, her careful attendance are not the perquisites
of royalty, but have reference to the propagation
of the species. Her sovereignty lies solely in this
supreme function. Her queenship is one of duties,
and not of rank.

A similar relation is detailed by Spence as existing in certain species of ants. Their king and
queen, their royal chambers, their capacious apart-
ments and extensive retinue only mean, when
divested of figure, the incidents that attend on the
continuation of the species. Much the same is
true in reference to the keeping of slaves by various
species of ants. It is simply an instance of a social

community constructed by the mutual ministration
of distinct species, and is brought about by the
very common practice among ants of stealing each
other's pupæ and larvæ. The words slaves and
masters are a mere gloss of language. The two
classes, like working ants and warriors, reciprocally
minister to each other. If this relation is one of
intelligence, it certainly is not one of mastery, for
the masters, if we also may be allowed this varnish
of speech, fall into the most abject dependence on
their slaves, and are as often ruled by them as they
rule them. In the dairy-keeping of the ants there
is much the same extravagance of phrase. The ant
profits by the secretion of the aphides, and has the
appetite to feed where food can be found. There
may be some reciprocal advantage accruing to the
aphides, but of this we are not certain. The relation goes no farther than an immediate appetitive
one, accompanied with a disposition to defend their
food. So a dog gnaws a bone, growls at his fellow
and buries it when through with it. An association of remote species for the benefit of one or
both is not uncommon in the animal kingdom.
The cuckoo laying its egg in the nest of other
birds ; the cow-bird in its association with kine ;
the trochilus and the crocodile ; birds of prey, like
kites and vultures, that attend, the weaker on the
stronger, are a few among many examples.

There seems to be no true leadership, no con-
certed plans, no designed concurrence of action between bees or between ants in carrying out their
purposes ; nor the opportunity in language proper

for any such pre-arrangement of effort. I do not mean to say that there are not many actions to which we may not, in facile interpretation, bring this rendering which is the shadow cast by our own powers on the life below us, but that careful observation establishes no real leadership or counsel among ants. We can, if we will, make the tree-tops whisper love to each other. Spence confirms the words of Solomon. They have "no captain, overseer or ruler." * This lack of guidance goes far to establish the essentially instinctive character of their social life. Such a life, so extended and complete, must have a decisive support somewhere, either in organic conditions or in counsel, or in both.

This brings us to what we believe to be the true explanation of the broad and varied instincts of the social insects. The egg, larva, chrysalis and insect stand organically united to each other. It is, therefore, nothing strange that the insect should provide for the egg and larva, the larva for the chrysalis and the insect. Here is a constitutional dependence which gives a basis for the longitudinal extension of organic action through the four steps of development. So the sexes are organically dependent on each other, and we explain by this fact their instinctive relations toward each other. In the same way we refer to organic facts those affections of parents for their young, which are called natural affections. They have

* Ibid. p. 330.

in animals a decisive force while they last, come to an abrupt conclusion, and are so blindly instinctive that the grossest tricks can be played upon them. Hamerton, in his Chapters on Animals, gives an instance in which the skin of her calf, very carelessly stuffed, was laid before the cow to draw. her attention while being milked. She proceeded to lick it with "the most delightful tenderness;" yet a little later, the fastenings giving way, she ate up the fodder it contained with entire composure. Natural affection flowed into a natural appetite without a ripple of intelligence.

Nor ought we to be so surprised as we are at the impressibility of the animal organism to involuntary stimuli, when we reflect that we, who have for generations resisted such tendencies, are yet occasionally subject to them in an unconquerable way. Impressions and aversions are fastened on our nervous system, sometimes by a single experience, which we never escape. Thus a child, eating to nausea of a coveted dish, ever afterwards loathes it. The very odor of a ship, or of the sea, is offensive to one who has suffered from protracted sea-sickness. The smell of varnish may suggest a funeral, or of thyme a graveyard.

If we take a community of bees or ants, we do not find that they are so many like distinct individuals, or pairs even, associated by inclination merely on terms of common and interchangeable services. They are organically interlaced with each other, complements of each other by peculiar functions and special labors that fall to them not by selection, but by constitution.   The queen of the hive is the one mother-bee, the drones are the males, and the working-bees the neuters.   Here the ordinary sexual relation, or one allied to it, is spread through the entire hive, shapes its economy, and divides its duties.   When we see, then, that the most marvelous instincts of the community turn on these same relations, the production of a queen, attendance upon her, supplying her place when lost, the slaughter of the drones, or the sparing of them when the hive is without a fertilized queen, the care for the young, we are led at once to believe that we have here the extension of an organic force, that ordinarily unites a single family, through an entire community, and that the social polity and good order of the hive are constitutional.   A single worker may go to another hive, but the hive is a society by virtue of functional distinctions allied to those between the sexes, and as decisive as they in controlling its life.   There is here a lateral extension of organic connections, allied to their longitudinal extension in the four stages of transformation.

Corresponding varieties of office and organization exist between the different occupants of an ant-hill.   As there are many species among ants, and much variety in their social economy, what is said in a general way of their habits and relations will not be equally true of them all.

We have in the ant-hill not only the king and the queen, or the two sexes, but extended secondary divisions of neuters quite beyond the simple relations of the hive.   Says Darwin : " The neuters

of several ants differ not only from the fertile females and males, but from each other, sometimes
to an almost incredible degree, and are thus divided
into two or even three castes. The castes, moreover, do not commonly graduate into each other, but
are perfectly well-defined, being as distinct as are
any two species of the same genus, or rather as any
two genera of the same family."* Says Sir John
Lubbock, in the article in the Popular Science
Monthly already referred to : " Under ordinary
circumstances an ant's nest, like a bee-hive, consists of three kinds of individuals ; workers or imperfect females, males, and perfect females.   *   *
In addition to the ordinary workers there is in some
species a second, or rather a third, form of female.*
In a Mexican species, besides the common workers,
there are certain others in which the abdomen is
swollen into an immense sub-diaphanous sphere.
These individuals are very inactive, and principally
occupied in elaborating a kind of honey.   In the
genus Pheidole there are also two distinct forms
without any intermediate gradations ; one with
heads of the usual proportion, and a second with
immense heads provided with very large jaws."†
The distinctions therefore between ants as workers
and soldiers are grounded in organic differences, and
their offices are not interchangeable.   Their relations to each are settled by constitutional development, and not by consent.   The soldiers swarm
out at once to defend the home, but quite decline

* Origin of Species, p. 230.   † Vol. xi. p. 40.

to repair it. On the other hand, no sooner is the attack over than "the laborers are in motion hastening in various directions towards the breach, every one carrying in his mouth a mass of mortar, half as big as his body, ready tempered. As fast as they come up each sticks its burden in the breach; and this is done with so much regularity," that though many thousands are engaged in the work they do not embarrass or delay each other.* The warriors have not only their powerful jaws, but their own secretion. This is no longer a glue with which to unite gravel into mortar, but a poisonous acid. "The combatants seize each other, rear on their hind legs, and instantly spurt their acid."† Shortly the ground is strewn with the dead, and the dead are covered with venom. Thus their method of fighting is as functional as the fight itself, and quite removed from conscious election.

When we add to these fundamental distinctions in the same community the introduction in different instances of wholly distinct species, now as co-partners, and now as the so-called slaves; and that all are wrought into one whole of mutually dependent parts, it seems plain enough that we have ample organic distinctions involved in the members of a community of ants to be made the basis of its wonderful social economy. The organic development in insects is strictly collective, as it is in many forms of lower life, and the individual cannot be regarded as consciously acting his part with those about him.

---

* Kirby & Spence's Entomology, p. 311.　　† Ibid. p. 327.

The nervous system of the higher insects is also sufficiently complete and centralized to be the medium of many complicated and combined stimuli. The development of their senses is such as to put them in active response to the outside world as immediately bearing on them. Hearing, a peculiarly intellectual sense, is dull; vision scarcely extends to remote objects, while their antennæ give them conditions of very delicate touch, and their sense of smell seems to be very acute, and in constant service. We infer this from the way in which bees and ants track each other, and follow their own track, and from the manner in which ants discover at once the place at which a fellow has met with disaster and turn back.

Without claiming it as fully established that every instinct has its organic basis, we think the conclusion is so certainly true in the majority of cases, and so probable in many more cases, as to make this the most rational explanation by far of all instinctive action. It puts, moreover, this form of life, or of intelligence, using the term concessively, in the closest dependence on that below it, and at the same time furnishes a new basis, a plastic medium for that directly above it. The instinct, as imitative of intelligent activity, can both open the way for this activity, and give ground before it.

The relations of instinct to evolution are obvious. The view now urged does not materially affect the question of the origin of the several forms of life, and the relation of their successive stages to each other. The organic foundations and their associated instincts may vary together, and the movement forward proceed under natural selection ; or the organs, and their instinctive functions, may receive positive increments in pre-arranged directions ; or the two methods may be parts of one method, which seems to us more probable. No very special considerations bearing on the doctrine of evolution arise at this point of the instincts. If we regard them as subtly enlarged organic action, they fall naturally into the general line of development.

The relation of instinct to intelligence is equally plain. Instinct first prepares the way for intelligence by securing safely the forms of life needful to a highly developed consciousness, and then slowly, as the incipient intelligence is ready to occupy the field, retires before it. It is like those lower forms of life, lichens and moss on the rock, that accumulate organic material, make ready for a higher growth, and are then excluded by it. Intelligence easily engrafts itself upon instinct, works its way into it, and so crowds it out. All that Wallace and others have said of the intelligence of birds in nidification and migration may well enough be true, and yet leave a large remnant of instinctive tendency. Indeed, this additional intellectual development breaking in on the instincts, is precisely what we have been urging. The uniformity in position, material and method of nesting belonging to each species may be referred to instinct, while special adaptations are explained by associative intelligence. The migrations of birds in their regularity, certainty, and precision, plainly imply an automatic impulse, but this impulse in its execution may suffer many modifications from passing impressions, and the introduction of an intelligent experience. We believe these departures from uniformity will be found to increase with the intelligence of the species ; they are very marked in some species, and very slight in others.

It ought not to surprise us that the organic system can take up at certain seasons of the year peculiar nervous stimuli securing appropriate action. Our own appetites are considerably affected by the seasons in the objects they crave, and some diseases, like hay-fever, have a very precise periodic character conformable to the year. The line which divides instinct from intelligence is a variable one, not only as between different species, but as between different individuals of the same species. When the higher faculties are present in any unusual degree, they necessarily cut into and modify the lower ones.

Habit is an image of instinct, though unlike it in origin. Habit may either be an undesigned tendency, fastened in the physical system by repetition, to renew certain states and forms of action ; or it may be skill, the power gained by practice to perform easily, automatically, some process more or less difficult. These induced states are superficially incorporated into the organic action. Dependencies are established which serve automatically, in the second class of habits, to sustain and carry forward the voluntary movement; or, in the first and more passive class, to impart quiet to the system by allowing it to drop into a familiar rut. These habits are then the deposit, designed and undesigned, of our voluntary life, and, as finally resting on impressions in the automatic constitution, are allied to instincts.

This connection of habits and instincts may in some instances be so close that the habit shall incorporate itself into an allied instinct, as an extension of it, and so pass with it to offspring by descent. The instinct in this case is the core, not the habit. Darwin has made facts of this order familiar. Dogs have acquired and transmitted peculiar hunting qualities. In these cases the acquisition was closely connected with vigorous organic tendencies, lying in the same direction, ready to take it up, incorporate it, and pass it on. Habits in the human family do not as a rule descend to children, because they do not penetrate deeply enough into the physical constitution. There is indeed a general belief that certain habits, primarily physical, do pass to offspring. Thus George Eliot, in Felix Holt, hints at an illegitimate relationship by a peculiar rubbing of the hands, which belongs to both father and son.

One may deepen by voluntary effort his method of breathing, and so, modifying his own lungs, transmit undoubtedly a superior functional activity. The peculiar connections of nerves and muscles due to our voluntary life, such a connection as that by which we repeat words by rote, do not secure a sufficiently deep constitutional basis to come under the law of inheritance. If they did, the conditions of rational, individual life would be pretty much wiped out, and intelligence would be self-destructive. The mind's action would be fore-stalled by chronic habits, by instincts. In propor-tion as intelligence softens instinct, and effaces its deep lines of division, does it limit the law of de-scent and restore the individual to his liberty.

Some have been led by this connection of habit and instinct to try to make the former the root of the latter. This is an entire subversion of the true order of evolution. Habits owe their force and their transmission to organic tendencies, not organic tendencies to habits. Habit can do noth-ing without an organic relation to build on. Dar-win very justly says : "It would be a serious error to suppose that the greater number of instincts have been acquired by habit in one generation and then transmitted to succeeding generations." *

But this leads us to our last consideration un-der instinct, its origin. What we have said goes far to settle the question. We have striven to show that it is a farther development of the organic life, and hence its origin and development are locked up with that life. G. H. Lewes urges the view that "instinct is lapsed intelligence ; that what is now the fixed and fatal action of organism was formerly a tentative and discriminating (conse-quently intelligent) action ; in a word, that what is

---

* Origin of Species, p. 206.

now a concrete tendency was formerly acquired experience." * Others incline to the same view, though few can have thoroughly considered all that is involved in it. Either we must narrow down instincts to a very restricted class of actions, or we must reco nize the organic element as fundamental in them. The greater share of them, all of them which contain an obvious organic dependence, can not be referred to experience. The spinning of the spider, or of the larva, the comb of the bee, and the paper of the wasp, cannot be the fruits of e perience merely, since they, in their formation, are only functions of peculiar organs. The organs can hardly be supposed to have existed without the function, waiting for experience to impart it ; nor could experience direct its use till the function was present. This explanation, therefore, cannot break in on the great central mass of instinctive facts.

Moreover, the theory virtually makes an instinctive life later in development than an intelligent one, since it is the ultimate product in which intelligence issues. Skill is higher than acquisition, but skill remains permeated with the voluntary, thoughtful tendency; can be taken up anew at any time by it, and so be wrought over into still higher results.   It is profoundly irrational to make instinct, through its entire breadth, subsequent to intelligence, and the product of it ; as much so as it would be to make organic life the offspring of instinctive life, because the latter modifies the former. It is a radical perversion of the relations of higher and lower, earlier and later, in the steps of development. The later must indeed modify the earlier, and so intelligence, while following instinct and steadily narrowing its field, may, in a limited degree incorporate itself in it ; but to seize on such secondary facts, and to strive to explain primary ones as a whole by them, is a method as mistaken as it would be to assert as a method that brick walls are built in sections from the top downward, because, occasionally, a wall already up is raised and supported from beneath.

In proportion as intelligence increases, instinct disappears ; yet if instinct lies last in the line of development, we should anticipate a time in which our conscious, voluntary life should be entirely swallowed up, or greatly narrowed, by an automatic, unconscious one. The fundamental order is the reverse of this ; instinct makes way for intelligence, and yields at its presence. Nor does the word, *lapsed*, in the definition, remove the difficulty. Instinct is not a decay of intelligence, nor a falling off of it. Habits badly formed and allowed a surreptitious organic basis may be this, but those rightly formed lie wholly in the line of rational development, and minister to it.

Few theories rest on a more narrow or a more mistaken rendering of facts, or are more subversive of fundamental relations than this that instincts are the products of experience, and so of intelligence. No profound insight into the order

of life is possible under such a view. The forces
of growth all come, like the buds that break the
soil, forcing themselves up from below. Each
stage enriches the soil in which the seeds of the
next are sown. Physical forces lie a broad stratum
under purely organic ones, organic forces sustain
in turn instinctive ones, while the three unite to
support the superincumbent activity of intelligence.

No safe theories can be wrung out of a few
facts that are considered in oversight of this leading relation. Though habit takes partially in rational life the place of instinct, the generic origin
of the two is very different. Habit is the striking
of intelligence downward into the subject organic
powers ; instinct is the stretching in development
of these organic powers outward and upward.

While our rational life is the last term in the
progression, it sends its succulent fibres to the
very bottom of things, as a present controlling
power.

CHAPTER VII.

ANIMAL LIFE AS ASSOCIATIVE.

In passing from instinctive to associative life, though the two are united by a broad over-lap, we meet with an absolutely new element, consciousness. Here is a term perfectly distinct from every one which has preceded it. It lies in advance of organic forces with the same decisive spacing which separates organic from purely physical forces. No effort to reduce this difference has met with the least success. When Taine tells us that mental facts are brain-phenomena seen from the inside, while viewed from the exterior they retain their physical appearance, he is talking in riddles, for the inside of a brain has no spiritual qualities above its outside.

Consciousness is the new condition or form of a new series of activities with whose phenomenal character we are most familiar, but of whose substance we have only that inferential knowledge which everywhere belongs to a search after essences. Little as we understand the relation of mental and physical facts to each other, mental facts still constitute our most immediate and complete knowledge. When we speak of thoughts, feelings and choices, all of them hourly passing through our consciousness, we are dealing with as plain and well-understood things as any to which we can possibly direct our speech. No feeling is known to us save as a conscious feeling, and when we speak of consciousness, we designate that which is the recognized condition of all our thinking, and that, therefore, which makes this language and all other language, this thought and all other thoughts intelligible to us. Nothing can be plainer in its nature than consciousness, since it is the ever present condition of all plainness. That which we mean by a plain truth is one which has found its way decisively into our consciousness. Consciousness being thus a perfectly primitive fact, the very form of knowledge, it is a loss of time to try to explain it farther, or to liken it to something else.

Consciousness, as the form of a new kind of being superinduced on organic and instinctive life, is the first condition of what we term associative life. Associative life is mental facts united in experience through memory. But consciousness is not itself being, but only the form of being. What, then, are the first phenomena to assume this form, to appear in consciousness? and when did these phenomena arise? We cannot answer these questions decisively. Conscious life, like organic life, doubtless arose slowly, and passed upward by slight increments. We cannot, however, easily trace its development, since the external signs of organic and instinctive life are readily mistaken for those of intelligence. Such great things are possible to instinctive life without consciousness, and consciousness when it comes so mingles with instinct and glimmers about it, that it is as impossi-

ble to separate the two as it is to give the dividing
line between light and darkness.

It is probable that sensibility to physical pain
and pleasure, and the appetites were the first mental facts to appear in consciousness. We argue
this from the fact that the conscious life evidently
roots itself in the organic life, grows out of it, and
is developed in completion of it. In this development purely organic stimuli are naturally enlarged
and supplemented by conscious appetites, additive
impulses working in the same direction with the
simply physical forces. An organic stimulus forti-
fied in consciousness by a reciprocal fact becomes
at once a sensibility and an appetite. We may
speak of it in a figurative way as a transfer of an
organic fact into consciousness. So extensively
have the appetites, the mental signs of organic
states, come to involve with us conscious activities,
that it is difficult for us to understand how perfectly pure organic stimuli can operate without
them; and how secondary conscious pain and
pleasure are to the processes which they now indicate to us and help us to control. The sensibilities are a kind of attachment to a mechanism which
may be quite complete within itself. These indi-
cators may not be, or they may exist to disclose
states with little control over them, or they may be
guides to very complete government. With us
they are often more than this, they are additive impulses leading to lines of action parallel with that
induced by the organic tendency but very much
in advance of it. The registration of an engine

instructs the engineer as to its present condition,
the way in which the forces involved are operating,
though the dial plates are not these forces. Such
a registration in pain, in thirst and hunger would
be a first link of connection between conscious and
unconscious activities, that were to take up common conditions of life and run on together.

This also is the order of development in human
life. The infant enters on a conscious activity
first through the sensibilities, the appetites, and is
trained for months almost exclusively in this school.
We need not insist on the greedy appetitive character of animal life, especially in its lower forms.

But the appetites must almost immediately be
supported in consciousness by the special senses.
An appetitive impulse alone in consciousness would
add nothing to the life-forces, but rather detract
from them. The unconscious organic stimuli would
still be left to work the muscular mechanism, and
the accompanying conscious state would be simply
a waste of energy, the burning of a taper that
guided no effort. Appetite, in order to become a
power acting consciously, must be associated with
other conscious facts, with one or more forms of
perception. The impulse has thus opened to it
directions in which it may expend itself; the conscious being begins to discriminate the things that
promote its pleasure, to associate them with appropriate action, and so consciously to secure its own
well-being. Amid germinating sensibilities, therefore, as farther rudiments of the coming conscious
life, there must arise the general and special

senses, sensibilities to facts supplementing those to pleasure and uniting with them in an experience.

We are to constantly bear in mind, however, that the organic conditions out of which appetites and sensations alike spring as additional conscious facts are deeply imbedded in the physical structure, and perform very fully their offices in an automatic way without any help from consciousness. The later relation is not the earlier one. The first and second terms are not co-extensive, though when both are present they coalesce in one result. This unity is secured by the prior sufficiency of the purely organic element, and by its later slow modification and enlargement through the voluntary element. The machine can run without an index or an engineer; and when the engineer comes, he cautiously unites his own action to previous action through this registration of states.

Conscious life must have not only two kinds of experiences as a condition of its associations, but also the power to unite and hold them in a systematic way. If the physical stimuli which underlie the sensations blindly, that is, automatically, direct the appetites, then both sensations and appetites as conscious factors are superfluous, idle consumptions of energy to be eliminated by natural selection. The palpitation of the stomach in hunger, or the fluttering of the heart in fear, is a simple disturbance of the vital mechanism, unless there is present, as the result of this conscious fact, some slight method of relief. Sensations and sensibilities must, then, be wrought together in a conscious experience, so that out of them there shall grow advantageous lines of action. Hence memory is a third primitive constituent in the unfolding of associative life, rising above and working with the organic life. Memory must also be recognized as an absolutely new and a purely mental fact, not as the shadow of a physical one. When the return of physical conditions calls forth memory, there is the same inscrutable transformation, or transfer in position, of the facts involved, from the physical to the mental world, from space to consciousness, that there is when vibrations become sensations, sound music, or floating particles odor. If not, then the conscious life fails again to be an additive force, and is once more a waste of previous forces. If the sensibility is simply the organic stimulus disclosed to itself as a craving, and the sensation the uncovering of the surrounding impulses, and memory a conscious experience which is no more than the repetition of inherent self-united nervous states, then the entire conscious life, and memory with it, become supernumerary, the empty reflection of the organic life, the shadow of processes going on, indeed, in the light, but which could with equal certainty have proceeded in the darkness. This chasing of empty images by each other in consciousness would thus throughout be an escape of steam in the air, a consumption that gives no return to the forces that sustain it. Such a life of consciousness would be in reference to the deeper organic life, a fungus to be worked against by all the laws of self-preservation.

If, then, we are to take the associative life for what it so obviously is, a higher, fuller life, giving expansion and power to the processes below it, we must make its elements, to wit, sensibilities, sensations and memory, real energies, constituting themselves in a living way into an independent experience. Memory thus becomes memory, a *power* that takes cognizance of the facts of consciousness in consciousness itself, and so *weaves* them into an experience which is not the mere counterpart of the facts themselves. The phenomena of conscious life cease to be regarded as the mere shadows of organic processes, as if a light had been placed in the midst of revolving wheels, and become the expression of a delightfully new energy, ready, under its own laws and in its own forms, to grow up out of the organic life, and in many ways to overshadow it. This relation and process find an image in the steady increase and growing influence of the cerebrum, the organ of consciousness, among the other cephalic ganglia. We have thus, then, three constituents of consciousness as the germs of mind, —sensibilities and appetites, sensations and perceptions, and memory.

How early does consciousness arise? If we interpret, as we are constantly doing, the experience of lower animals by that of higher ones, we should answer, with the very commencement of animal life. Indeed, nothing but conventional sentiment would prevent our attributing, under this method, a feeble consciousness to some plants. If, however, we reason from the character of the nervous sys-

tem, which is undoubtedly the sole organ of consciousness, and from the stages in development at
which a conscious experience can enter as a profitable factor, we shall be inclined to believe that
consciousness especially characterizes the Vertebrata, and appears first in the higher Articulata and
Mollusca. The phenomena of consciousness undoubtedly increase greatly in vigor. and in value
as we pass up through the Vertebrata, and this form
of activity is in its governing relations collected
and specialized in the cerebrum.

We can hardly suppose a divided consciousness
in the same animal, as there is no experience to
guide us in such a supposition, and as the oneness
of organic action and interests would not readily
admit of it. So long, therefore, as the nervous
system exhibits no controlling centre, but is gathered sporadically into several centres, the rudimentary senses having different nervous connections, we have no reason to suppose that its
action is attended with consciousness. Not till
cephalization is so far complete as to make the head
a controlling centre of nervous phenomena, have
we the preparation for a conscious life, which can
maintain its unity, and so accumulate a valuable
experience by virtue of coherent and continuous
phenomena. Indeed, in the Vertebrata, whose mode
of life is undeniably and preëminently conscious,
as compared with that of other sub-kingdoms, we
have not merely cephalization, but distinct ganglia,
the cerebrum, as the special organ of consciousness,
giving it a force and unity of action not approached

elsewhere. We might reason to the entire absence of consciousness in lower animals from the absence of this organ of intelligence. This argument, however, would be unsafe, as a function before it is fully specialized in one organ, is often spread through allied organs. Lower ganglia, in the absence of higher ones, undoubtedly have a more extended service, precisely as many pigment-spots may do partially the work of two complete eyes. There are also present in the cuttle-fish ganglia which may be homologous to the cerebrum. Yet there seems good ground to believe that consciousness arises slowly with the increase of that unity in the nervous system which puts it under the control of a single centre, gathers the senses about that centre, and knits the organic life as closely as does consciousness our intellectual activity. Certainly from the fact that in the only region in which we have a direct knowledge of the phenomena of consciousness, they owe their unity to one supreme organ, we should infer that the two terms of development, nervous and intellectual, have the connection now indicated ; that consciousness becomes the specialized function of the cerebrum from a previously weak, vague and confused form.

We also reach the same conclusion from the development of the senses. Those which, like the senses of touch and smell, are close and narrow in their action, may readily operate in full force automatically. So may the sense of sight, when it is a simple discrimination between light and darkness, or the condition of adjustment to things just at hand; and the sense of hearing, when it is a recognition of the jar of vibrations, rather than a distinguishing between sounds, leading to a distinction of their sources. Sight, in its advanced forms, preëminently ministers to the conscious life. By virtue of the distance and complexity of the phenomena offered, it calls for an extended selection between them, courting the aid of experience. Growth in the range and clearness of vision is doubtless accompanied by a corresponding enlargement of consciousness, ready to take in and serviceably combine these numerous facts. We should hence infer in the higher Articulata and Mollusca a dawning consciousness as the first effort to economize superior senses.

The sense of hearing, even more than that of sight, is complex and intellectual in its later facts, and implies, therefore, if these are present in any good degree, a clear consciousness supporting and interpreting them. This sense more than any other owes its value to the mental activities that lie back of it, and rapidly falls away with any weakness of the intellectual faculties. What, how much, and how we hear, as well as what we see, are settled almost wholly by the conscious life, and these two senses can become full and intellectually complex only in connection with a deepening and enlarging consciousness. These senses have no fuller stream than is sufficient to float the life that rides on them. When, therefore, Sir John Lubbock shows that the higher insects, as ants, are poor listeners; and with their out-standing eyes have but narrow vision, he brings great limitations to their intelligence.* In all that region of animal life in which these two senses are greatly restricted in development, and still further restricted in use, we infer a narrow consciousness, that stands on no terms of comparison with that of the upper Vertebrata.

We also conclude, in a general way, that the instinctive and the associative life bear an inverse ratio to each other. Our knowledge where it is fullest in the higher Vertebrata establishes this relation. There is in man but a very small remainder of instincts, while they rapidly increase as we pass downward. This conclusion is also involved in the very nature of the case, as instincts and experience tend mutually to replace, and so to exclude, each other. The instinct, in its own range, supplies the place of experience ; while experience once present narrows down the range of instinct. We would, therefore, conclude that insects, with which instincts culminate, have a relatively narrow experience, most of their action taking place in absolute darkness, or in the light of a glimmering intellectual day.

The clearest proof of consciousness in doubtful territory is memory. This faculty is the basis of experience, and not till it has been obtained can the facts of consciousness, if any are present, begin to be organized into knowledge. The action of memory is also more readily discriminated from

* Popular Science Monthly, vol. xi. p. 51.

automatic action than is the conscious from the unconscious use of the senses. While instinct may take on a periodic form, somewhat allied to recollection, true memory can be distinguished by the variability and precision of its action. When a bee returns to the same place for honey on successive journeys, till all is removed, and then at once discontinues its visits, it is safe to suppose that the amount of the food is present to its memory. Yet careful observation exposes much confusion in the minds of bees and ants, and many futile efforts through the lack of memory. They seem to take little note of direction as direction, to be easily led out of the way by a change of scent, and to be entirely baffled if this is lost. Bees and ants not only have little or no power to impart to each other the locality of food, they themselves retrace their own steps instinctively, not constructively. Bees search flowers much at random ; and in the motion of ants there is much of that irregular, vacilating movement which belongs to a hound that has lost the scent. This instinctive control of a familiar path is seen in higher animals than bees. A gopher was filling his nest with straw. He had moved repeatedly in a straight line from one heap to the mouth of his hole. Disturbed in his course, he turned aside and discovered a second heap much nearer. He helped himself and returned to his nest. When again he made his appearance he still followed the longer and more familiar way, without seeming to recall his last experience.

The weakness of memory in bees is indicated by

facts given by Kirby and Spence. " If during their absence their old hive be taken away, and a similar one set in its place, they enter this last; and, if it be provided with brood-comb, contentedly take up their abode in it, never troubling themselves to inquire what has become of the identical habitation which they left in the morning, and with the inhabitants of which, if it be removed to fifty yards distance, they never resume their association."* This is a very significant fact, when taken with another fact already referred to, the great indifference which bees, and frequently ants, show to the fortunes of their fellows. Affections are fed by recollections, and where there is little affection there is little memory, and a vanishing experience. The general indifference of bees to their social surroundings, which prepares them for the slaughter of the drones, also shows them to feel but faintly the tender touches of memory.

In the Vertebrata, the great field of associative life, there is undoubtedly a steady increase as we pass upward in the number and variety of facts that occupy consciousness. A special organization, a peculiarly vigorous sense, as of scent in the hound, or of vision in the vulture, may give varieties of experience, but the law of general progress in conscious facts is not thereby materially modified. The tendency even here, however, is unduly strong to transfer our enlarged activities to our mute friends below us, and to make a fact in their experience the

* Entomology, p. 565.

centre of thoughts and affections similar to those that would cluster about it in ours. The sun's rays may steal without observation through the dry air, or they may trace in all directions on its vapors paths of radiance; the light of consciousness may be barren to the mind, or bring with it many mystic visions. These profound differences in the inner experiences of distinct grades of life will appear more and more clearly as we contrast associative and rational action. We argue directly and mercifully this limited light of the mind in animals from the evidently reduced effects of suffering. We are to remember that purely automatic action presents the same visible and even audible signs which belong to complete consciousness. When the divided angle-worm wriggles and writhes in the path, there may seem to be acute suffering along its entire length, yet the probability remains that both halves are alike unconscious of the injury done them. When the head of a hen is cut off, the child bestows its sympathy on the convulsive throes of the body, yet it is the head, fallen behind the log, that calls for attention, if either part claims it. The heart may throb for "some time" after it has been taken from the body, but it indicates thereby only the expenditure of a remnant of nervous energy. "Impressions which in normal conditions would excite groans or cries, and also painful sensations, under certain degrees of anæsthesia elicit merely the groans and cries," with no indication of conscious suffering.*

* Functions of the Brain, p. 69.

A careful observation of animals shows that in-
juries are far less distressing to them than to man.
Insects make light of the loss of a limb. Dogs will
continue a battle with unflagging courage when
fatal wounds have been inflicted that would have
quickly sapped the nervous energy of man. I have
seen a hen, whose leg had been stepped on and
broken by a cow, hasten up on the protruding bone
the moment she was released from under the foot
of the stolid beast, in order to claim afresh her
share of the meal the larger brute was devouring.
Horses draw all day on galled shoulders with comparatively little show of suffering. A reduction of
consciousness, and so of pain, undoubtedly attends
on a less highly organized nervous system. The associative life is as much less sensitive as it is less
penetrative than the rational life which lies above
it ; the two are different sides of the same fact. Nor
does this general dulness of feeling exclude unusual
acuteness of perception in single directions. The
stimuli in these cases, as of odor, may be largely
automatic. The dog does not take up in terms of
knowledge the greater part of his organic discriminations. Connections in the human mind, origin-
ally conscious and voluntary, may become so obscure
and automatic as to take effect against the express
purpose and best knowledge of the person involved,
as shown in table-tipping. An anticipation of a result will easily work its way through the sub-conscious mechanism of the human body to its own realization. With the facts of mind-reading and kindred facts before us, we have no occasion to sur-

round, as we do, the mental activities of brutes with the clear light of consciousness. In most animals the mental revelation is to the organic movement which underlies it, what the feeble flash is to the powerful electric current.

. It is very difficult for us to conceive the form which the associative life assumes when separated from rational insight. We suppose it most nearly to resemble a distinct, realistic dream, in which objects present themselves, and events move on, with no control or reflection on our part. The chief feature of this life, as in the dream, is the manner in which the attention is absorbed by the objects before the mind, the way in which they come and go of their own impulse, while the feelings preserve an unbroken flow with them. The passing moment is a charmed circle beyond which the thoughts travel not, no matter what things may flow through it. The associative life deals with the concrete, with an eternal now and here. Other experiences may modify this experience, but they do it directly, associatively by a sensational term before the mind. All is changeable surface, flickering shadows in this shallow light, and the thoughts raise no questions of the hereafter.

The dog presents perhaps the highest form of this life. And the highest attitude of his life is his affectionate absorption into the experiences of man. His master is to him a physical gnomon, whose shadows follow each other almost mechanically on the dial-plate of his existence, and mark all its periods. When he pines for his master, it is not for an abstract, ideal conception, but for a well-known compound of qualities, odors, actions, whose absence, like that of a meal, is here and now felt. His affections are no more of a transcendent character than are hunger and thirst, and survive ill-usage as these appetites survive bad food and poor water. The associative life is preëminently direct and concrete in its objects. It abides steadfast, like an island in a river, or a ruling impression in a revery, while the world floats by it, and acts insensibly on it.

We are thus led to believe that there is at most but a dim consciousness in the Mollusca and Articulata, and one confined to the higher genera. We infer it from a scattered nervous system in the lower members of the sub-kingdoms, from very restricted organs of sense, from the weakness of memory even in the higher orders, and from the universal presence, extent and strength of instinct. In the Vertebrata we reason more certainly, since we have a recognized organ of consciousness, the cerebrum, whose development we can easily trace. We start again without consciousness in the Amphioxus, and pass a long way up through its very feeble and its secondary development, till at length, in the higher animals, the cerebrum is the primary nervous organ, and consciousness is the constructive force of the external life, and in man is the condition of a wholly new interior life.

We need to see more distinctly the three elements of which this form of intelligence is made up. Appetites and sensibilities are its first term :

keen appetites, since they spring from a vigorous physical system, kept in healthy tension, are over-shadowed and embarrassed by few other impulses, and are restrained by no conscientious scruples ; quick sensibilities, since the whole nervous mechanism, like a silent bell, waits for the few strokes of attention that time records on it. The overbearing influence of the organic life, and the entire absence of the rational element, are seen in the limits which these energetic animal appetites set themselves, both as to the kind and quantity of food. Though the animal occasionally seems to be caught in error or in gluttony as to his food, it is usually in appearance only. There, is in some animals, as in snakes, a physical elasticity which enables them to put long intervals between their meals, and to eat large amounts. The decision and safety which characterize the appetites of animals must give them also great positiveness and concentration as intellectual elements. They must for the moment as perfectly absorb the mind as they do the body.

The same is true of constitutional sensibilities leading to activity or to rest; to courageous on-slaught, cunning retreat, or timid flight ; to attachments and repulsions between species, and between individuals of the same species ; to natural affections, blazing up under provocation into fierce anger, and dying down as the danger retires into fondling love ; to fidelities of one sort or another, yet so strong that faithfulness may find its best image in a horse or a dog. In these sensibilities there are the same decisive limits, the almost complete exclusion of one thing by another, the same concentration of experience in the phase through which it is passing. The life of the brute is painted in a few simple colors, the life of man is laid in with many depths of color, all struggling to the surface in the final result. In these simple, vigorous impulses, not all present in any one animal, nor present in numbers at any one time to soften and distract each other, we get elements of the simplest character, associatively compounded into a few strong tendencies. We have a few forces that will push unhesitatingly and energetically in the ways open to them.

Passing these active elements, the second set of constituents are varied and keen senses. The discriminations of the senses have no known limits. They may fall much below the power they show in man, and they may greatly overpass it. That perception in animals does, in single directions and in organic force, outstrip perception in man is evident. The most familiar example is that of scent. The unhesitating and rapid pursuit by a dog of his master, even through a thoroughfare, guided by the odor of his footsteps, indicates an acuteness of smell of which we know nothing. Two things, however, are to be remembered. Such a perception as this widens but a very little the mental horizon, and serves rather to take the place of than to awaken intellectual action ; and that this keenness of one or two senses has universally an immediate reference to the habits of the animal, and serves simply to impress upon it more strongly a narrow type of character. In other words, these keen senses are not general but special instruments, not intellectual but physical agents ; they run in a narrow rut, not in an open field, are not so much broad as far-reaching, do not so much rise high in intellectual light as sink deep in organic structure. The way in which these restricted sensibilities and keen senses would unite in a few complete and decisive phases of action is very plain. The whole intellectual realm would be quickly beaten by them into a limited number of narrow paths, and have in all its open spaces no further significance. The mind of the simple-hearted brute thus stands in complete contrast with the mind of man ; the interstitial spaces of primary thought all occupied by modifying conditions; the canvas covered with the elaborate facts of life. Such senses as ours would overwhelm with what they give a constructive power less vigorous than ours.

The third element is memory. This may be and often is very retentive in the animal. There is no reason why it should not be, for the range of objects is restricted, and these objects are closely associated with daily well-being. Concentration and reiteration, the two conditions of impressing the memory, pass in the experience of the brute into an extreme form. The narrow wheel cannot fail to rut the ground over which it travels. Out of these two elements, with this strong combining power, there must arise an associative life which shall show many striking attainments, all the more striking from their detached, isolated character. A series of memoriter judgments will be woven together by experience, which, when resting back on full organic impulses, and large instincts, will make a very complete, and, in its own grade, a very self-sufficing life.

When we speak of memoriter or associative judgments, we are using the words in an accommodative way. Such a union by memory of things that have often appeared together in experience is not properly a judgment. A judgment involves a rational insight into the relations of subject and predicate, and a direct, conscious union of the two in a specified connection. A memoriter judgment is only a *quasi* judgment, the union of two impressions in consciousness referable to the simple fact that they have been so united in experience. We term such a union of ideas indifferently a memoriter or an associative judgment, though the basis of it is exclusively the power of memory. An associative judgment is likely to be more decisive, and have a more immediate governing power, than a rational one. When the dog smells the step of his master, the odor acts as energetically in restoring the conception of the master as would vision itself; when the hunter infers the whereabouts of game by a rational interpretation of signs, he feels uncertain in proportion as he gets away from the direct testimony of the senses. It is impossible in man to separate fully the memoriter and the rational elements in judgments—the inference and the association. In proportion, however, as the reflective life becomes vigorous, associations are pushed into the background; and, on the other hand, in the degree in which the activity of the senses is uppermost, do the associative judgments of the animal, as in savages and hunters, prevail. Let us see how such associations are formed in the experience of the brute.

The leopard steals cautiously upon a herd of deer: animals swift, timid, with a quick scent and alert ear. The leopard must needs approach them, therefore, very slowly, silently and secretly from the leeward. He must not snap a dead branch, or stir a living one. He must crouch low and glide stealthily toward his prey. How plainly organic structure, instinctive tendencies, and acquired associations work together in the final result. The crouching movement and the sudden terrible spring are organic; the caution, the patience, the sharp attention are organic and instinctive tendencies, shaped and confirmed by long use; the avoidance of crackling under-brush, and the approach against the wind, are associative judgments. How inevitably would experience in an eager, alert, sensitive organism issue in these and in like items of knowledge. The broken branch, the sharp sound, the instantly startled deer would form one clear, indelible image, an associative judgment not to be forgotten.

We are constantly to remember that the connection of the two things, noise and failure, does not arise in the animal from reasoning, nor lead to reasoning as it would do in man. The simplest fact with us may provoke a series of thoughts, and as a fact get its interpretation and intellectual force from this tracing of causes. Our reflective powers, like ambient light, begin at once to play about every succession of events. Reasons, causes with us underlie everything. We do not allow circumstances simply to follow each other, but we begin at once to put under them these connections of the mind. Not thus is it in purely associative judgments. Two facts, with no discussion of reasons or causes, with none of these satellites of the mind to revolve about them, are picked up and united in memory, so that the first brings with it as an image the second. The connection between them is the connection of a dream, of a panorama, and not one of reasons. We should be able the more easily to understand this purely phenomenal flow of events, since our dreams give us so familiar an example of it.

The only difficulty in these associative judgments is to understand how the animal, in a complicated experience, singles out the two things which hold a practically valuable relation to each other, and unites them in memory to the exclusion of other things. What is the force of selection? In the specific case, how does the leopard, without reflection, connect the crackling of a dry twig with the flight of the deer, since other facts besides these two must at the same time be present in its consciousness?

In the first place, under an imperious appetite and searching senses, the consciousness of a beast of prey, in the exertion of his powers, is much more limited and exclusive than it would be in

man, and those items alone in it receive attention
or come into prominence, which immediately bear
on the action going forward. This is as inevitable
as that a muscle being excited should receive the
strain and rise on the surface. We may liken the
results in the memory to those on the plate of the
photographer, when the light falls clearly on two
portions only of the objects present. These would
immediately stand forth in close association, while
other parts would fall quite away. What is termed
the sagacity of brutes lies just here, the bold relief
which they by special appetites, affections, senses,
give to particular portions of their experience, and
the degree, therefore, in which they practically,
not reflectively, analyze it, and recombine it for
their own ends. A stupid brute not only receives
faint impressions, he receives uniformly (which is
much more important) faint impressions, hence, its
experience remains in limbo, precisely as it found
it. A series of sensations pass by, but none are
selected and combined ; there is no associative
union between related parts. Let effects be regis-
tered in hungry appetites, lively sensibilities ; and
let the answering causes be recorded in alert senses,
and a strong ray of light, falling on each member of
the judgment, fastens it in the memory, and the
memory holds it tenaciously for future service.
Thus the brute is wiser by a fixed association, a
working principle, than it was before. Nor need
we represent this process as at all a mechanical
one. It has a large organic element, and also a
decisively intellectual one. While different objects

make different constitutional appeals to the brute, there is none the less in the perception a true mental quality. To this is added a direction of attention, and a treasuring of results in memory. In dreams, though we often seem to control nothing, objects are not equally impressed on the mind, and a central current of events finds a channel through the automatic panorama.

If we consider the second and more difficult associations in the example referred to, that which leads the leopard to approach against the wind, we shall find its formation slower, perhaps, but hardly less certain. We cannot suppose the leopard, with a sudden recognition of causes, virtually to say to himself: "If I come near on this side, these deer are sure to detect my presence by odor and sound, but if I slip around and steal up against the wind, I shall easily accomplish my purpose;" we believe rather that his instincts and experience combine to issue in this method, a method transferred by descent, example and kindred experience to his offspring. The leopard himself, guided as much by odor and sound as by sight, would, in much the majority of cases, become aware of the neighborhood of deer when they were to the windward of him. The same circumstances that concealed him from the deer would disclose the deer to him. His approach, therefore, would usually be made, as a matter of fact simply, from this side, and would be frequently successful. On the other hand, when he came with the wind, the deer in the majority of cases would be aware of his nearness before he recognized them, and in case of an onslaught would easily escape, from the early alarm. Thus so general an experience would rapidly fasten itself in the mind, or, rather in the memory, of the leopard, that successful hunting is to be done against the wind. The wind, moreover, is not an obscure and secondary agent to the senses of an animal, but, laden with sounds and odors, is a primary fact. Let food be habitually found in the movement up a stream and not down it, and a fish even could hardly miss so palpable a fact. We forget that our very tendency to reason leads us to leave events much less carefully analyzed by the senses than does the eager animal, whose powers are all taken up by the senses. The thing that is profitable to him is the thing that speedily gets foremost in his impressions. Grant an eager, sensitive organism, running freely in the lines of constitutional impulses, and a complicated and valuable experience would at once begin to grow up, and find easy transmission by physical and social descent.

The organic and the instinctive elements which underlie such an experience, striking up into it and mingling with it, would often give very startling results, seeming to imply rare intelligence. We can see, also, how the associative experience, springing up as an expansion of the instinctive life, and itself a more complete and flexible adaptation, would begin at once to react on that life, first give it pliancy and breadth, and then absorb it in itself. The blind instinct would slowly yield before the coy, observant intelligence; and this power, more and more accumulating the conditions of growth, would spread over the debatable ground of action by which the animal adapts himself to his environment. Sharp appetites, quick senses and a ready memory would inevitably bury under a growing experience of associative judgments the primitive work of instinct, and themselves become the soil in which the seeds of a clear, reflective life could be planted.

That associative life, with slowly accumulated products of knowledge, in many cases wrought into and held firm by instincts, is coëxtensive with the higher animal life, and can satisfactorily explain its phenomena, there is but little doubt. Indeed, in discussing the sufficiency of this exposition, we may well remember that there is an influential school of philosophy, which would give much greater extension to this view, and make all intelligence in origin and development associative. The subtile way in which an instinct may linger on, and shape associative experience, is seen in the tendency to feign death, so common in lower animals, reappearing in higher ones; or in the deception practiced so frequently by birds, and by birds so unlike as an ostrich and a partridge, that of fluttering along the ground to attract attention and aid the retreat of young.

The lower animals mislead each other, and are easily misled, by stillness. The gopher will stand perfectly quiet on its hind legs, and is then readily mistaken for a stick. On the other hand, if one remains perfectly still, his presence soon ceases to alarm this animal. The action in both

cases is an adjustment to sensation, not to judgment. The gopher does not seem to recognize
man as man, but only to observe him as a moving animal.

The grounds on which we would contrast animal
life sharply with human life, the one as merely
associative, the other as rational, are many, but
centre about two considerations. There is a radical
difference between associative development and
rational development. Association requires for the
construction of its relations a comparatively narrow
and unchangeable experience. While the bold relief given by limited, sharp senses and a few absorbing impulses is an essential part of an associative
experience, its practically serviceable relations must
also be impressed on the memory by frequent rehearsal. A rapidly changing experience would in
turn rapidly efface each succeeding lesson. Hence
uniformity is added to narrowness as another feature of this form of life. On the other hand, the
rational impulses are peculiarly trammeled by fixed
relations. Reason is constantly called on to break
through first impressions and conventional habits,
and substitute for them fresh, inherent dependencies of its own tracing. Ratiocination is favored by
large and varying experience, and is struggling constantly to escape the ruts into which human
thought, the moment it loses vigor, is sinking. It
breaks up old associations, readily forms new ones,
and endeavors to make movement in all directions,
as on a broad, smooth plain, easy and habitual.
The more man rises into full possession of his own

powers, the more he gains this freedom ; the more he sinks back into animal life, the more he loses it, and feels the restored force of habit.

Animal life, through its whole range, shows unmistakably in the character and growth of its knowledge the inflexible features of association. Each species has its own food, its own habits, its own powers, and these sustain each other in a complete but narrow development. The knowledge of the species grows out of the experience incident to its fixed method of life, and rarely transcends it. We look for nothing in the brute which its own circumstances do not directly call for, and may not have taught it. We shall not be able to trace the formation of each association, any more than we can anticipate each accidental conjuncture of events, but the association lies as an easy possibility in the surrounding facts. We see no traces of those reflective processes which gather their harvests in all fields. That experiences so intense and restricted in themselves, yet so varied between themselves, should show many wonderful instances of the happy conjunctions called cunning, is a matter of course. If this craft, however, is to be ascribed to reflection, it would be very strange that reflection, which travels all paths equally well, should in each instance move in a single path so freely, and yet never get beyond it. As a rule, animals are made more dull by domestication, civilization. This would be a surprising result under the supposition of rational powers, but an inevitable one under association. The experience of the domestic

animal is reduced in variety, and much softened in
the intensity of its incentives; hence it is less
intellectual, especially with well-fed, well-cared-for
brutes. Turn the horse out on the common, and
his powers will be refreshed, and his cunning re-
vivified. The dog which is taken into close communion with his master, and kept active in the field
and the wood, forms naturally an exception to this
rule ; as also does the horse under like conditions. But the surprising thing after all is that
animals gain so little from human, that is from
rational, intercourse. Some domestic animals, as
the goose and the hen, are excessively dull. I have
known a fowl to be removed each night to its
appropriate perch for three months, and still not
take the hint. The stupid way in which a hen will
adhere to her nest without eggs, and often after
violent dissuasion, furnishes an instance of a wasted
remnant of instinct, lingering in a perverted form
in the midst of an associative life that should have
abolished it. Thus a rugged table-rock looms up on
a plain, the only remaining trace of a complete
stratum.

The instruction of brutes shows with equal decision the associative character of their knowledge.
The training of an ox is typical of all *training*, and
instruction in the animal kingdom is training. The
kind, uniform hand secures docility, and slowly im-
presses the will of the master. A few well-learned
lessons, instinctively wrought into the constitution,
makes a liberal education. Says Hamerton, and it
is the experience of all who have to do with animals:

" The way to educate a horse is to do as Franklin did in the formation of his moral habits, that is, to aim at one perfection at once; and afterwards, when that has become easy from practice, and formed itself into a habit, to try for some other perfection."* This is wisdom as applied to the brute, wisdom as applied to action of the nature of skill or habit in man, but folly as applied to that intellectual correctness or moral integrity which demands to be at once pervasive in thought and in action.

The chief difficulty in training always lies in bringing the two things to be associated up contiguously in the attention of the animal. For this, even in the most skilful handling, accident must be in part relied on, and the astuteness of the trainer shows itself in discerning each approach to the happy coincidence, and availing himself at once of it. If the knowledge to be imparted lies in the general direction of instinctive tendencies, the work is comparatively easy, and its results permanent; but if it lies to one side of these, as learning in a pig, the labor is great and the results superficial. The knowledge of the brute is, in that case, far more in the master than in himself.

The limits of knowledge in animals also indicate its associative character. One syllogism clearly constructed may be said to contain the entire logic; one thought distinctly entertained implies full rational powers in normal activity. After that, progress is only a question of time and opportunity.

---

* Chapters on Animals, p. 82.

Associative knowledge, on the contrary, ends abruptly. No one connection involves another, and every connection must arise in daily experience, and be implanted by it. Training, when most successful, bears no comparison with education when most difficult. Take the case of the rational powers of Laura Bridgman, shut up, as in a prison, in a body deaf, dumb and blind, the spirit inaccessible to the world without it, and without access to it. Yet, when the obstructing walls had been undermined, and a single obscure entrance to the signs of thought had been found in touch, after a little the gates of knowledge were unlocked, began to stir on their heavy hinges, and anon swung slowly open. The brute with the liveliest senses is labored over and labored with, and in spite of all attainments the final impression is of the impenetrable nature of the barriers that cut him off from all true comprehension.

Mr. Spalding, whose careful observation of instincts has excited so much interest, draws attention to the close connection of associative knowledge and organic tendency, and the limits put upon the one by the other. "In still further confirmation of the opinion that such wonderful examples"—he is speaking of the skill of a young turkey in catching a fly—"of dexterity and cunning are instinctive and not acquired, may be adduced the significant fact that the individuals of each species have little capacity to learn anything not found in the habits of their progenitors. A chicken was made, from the first and for several months, the

sole companion of a young turkey. Yet it never
showed the slightest tendency to adopt the admirable art of catching flies that it saw practiced
before its eyes every hour of the day. The only
theory in explanation of the phenomena of instinct
that has an air of science about it, is the doctrine
of Inherited Association. Instinct in the present
generation of animals is the product of the accumulated experiences of past generations."* We have
already commented on the insufficiency of this doc·
trine of inherited association to explain the primary
facts of instinct, and the very relation here pointed
out by Mr. Spalding strengthens the criticism. If
the associative knowledge lies in the direction of
the instinctive tendency, and adds itself to it, it can
hardly be the germ of that tendency. The lichen
grows and decays on the rock; the moss follows the
lichen; the fern the moss; flowers and shrubs the
ferns. Do lichens, mosses, ferns and shrubs make
the rock? Do they not rather slowly disintegrate
it? Does the moss make the lichen, or the fern
the moss, because they work together for a time?

The promptness also of the action of the brute
betrays its automatic character. Reflection is
slow, hesitates between several methods; association is instant and pushes on in one way. The
brute, in the hour of danger, is unembarrassed by
thought, by a half dozen suggestions none of which
promise success. His measures are taken on the
spur of a controlling association, and so have the
additional chances which belong to decision.

* Nature, vol. vi, p. 486.

The fact to which attention has now been drawn, that the knowledge of the animal in its kinds, functions, limits and methods is associative, not rational, is far more significant in proof of the character of a great phase of life than are detached instances of sagacity, which, under any view, must necessarily arise, are often badly stated in form, are obscurely understood in their instinctive and experiential surroundings, and owe their argumentative value to the gloss of an interpretation reflected on them from human experience. We can scarcely be mistaken as to these general features of intelligence in its two forms, we may be most easily mistaken, nay, we can hardly escape mistake, as to the precise way in which any particular act of sagacity has arisen.

We come now to our second great fact in this discussion, and to the inferences involved in it, to wit, that animals never use language. In saying this, we do not mean that animals do not many of them often, and some of them constantly, communicate to each other their present feelings as concrete states. They cannot avoid doing this. To feel fear is to show it. They are emotional facts, and as such reveal themselves to their fellows. We mean to say that language in its proper, primary office, that for which as articulate speech it is alone necessary, the expression and retention of abstract qualities and relations, is wholly unknown to animals, and cannot be taught them.

We are to drop out from language all the natural signs of emotion, the means by which a

present feeling directly discloses itself, actions, atti-
tudes, inarticulate sounds, and confine our attention
to utterances which originate purely in a rational
process, and call for it in their interpretation.   It
is evident that much which is properly enough
called language, will not, under this limitation,
concern us.   It is not the signs by which forces
actually at work express themselves,—for in this
connection clouds are the language of storms, muscular movements of vital forces, and changes in
the features of the emotions—that constitute the
distinctive substance of language; but those articulate sounds and written characters which, with
no power in themselves, convey thought, being assigned by the mind itself in its use of them that
office.   The neighing of horses, the lowing of
herds, the barking of dogs, the clucking of hens,
the singing of birds are all excluded from speech,
since they are the direct utterance of feeling.
Cats, that crouch opposite each other in a court-
yard, and frighten the night with unearthly sounds,
are not interlocutors.   When Hamerton says of
the dog, that he converses with his master by
means of his eyes and his ears and his tail, nay
rather by every muscle of his body, he is making
this converse of precisely the same character as
that which we hold with every sensitive object in
nature.   What we are in search of is a language
that requires neither eye nor ear nor tail to utter
it.   When an ox obeys a word of command, there
is in this obedience no more comprehension of
language than when he is quickened by a goad.

While natural and conventional signs are with men constantly gliding into each other, there is none the less so radical a division between them, that the latter imply quite different powers from the former. The clown and the novelist, the tuneless peasant and the tuneful poet, are distinguished from each other by different degrees of development at this very point, the former *have* character and utter it in action, and gurgle it out in monosyllables ; while the latter clearly *conceive* character, and so express it in flowing speech. Written language is a purer product of the linguistic powers than spoken language.

Certain cabalistic characters are on the parchment. Can the eye run over them and turn them into conceptions ? If so, that mind is rationally· endowed, since here is a rational not an associative link that it renders ; if it cannot do this, it is because its more clumsy faculties cannot reach the devices of mind. Can the dog read the guideboard and direct his steps accordingly ? The tricks of spelling, even of translation from language to language, to which dogs have been trained, furnish one of the most absolute proofs against their rational powers. The labor of such instruction and acquisition is incalculably greater than would belong to the rational acquisition of such power ; and that this apparent knowledge should remain after all a pains-taking trick of association, a play of signs and countersigns, is the most positive proof that there is no spark of rational comprehension in the dog's mind. Here are the best possible conditions to evoke it if it were present. The results of the laborious discipline are indeed surprising, yet they are of the most isolated, barren character, a mere surface gloss of associations, a wisdom that expires the moment any one of its critical conditions fails. This fact shows to us most plainly that the brilliant feats of natural cunning rest, like these acquired ones, on the same low plane of an associative experience.

There is no occasion for language proper, and no ability to acquire it, without the power of abstraction, itself an act of judgment. So long as the mind deals only with concrete things, their images and the impressions left by them on the memory, they themselves serve as a sufficient attachment to experience, and the only attachment of which it can avail itself. A language of conventional signs is to such an intelligence as steep and inaccessible as the face of a wall to a vine without foot-tendrils. The moment, however, the mind reaches an abstract relation, separates the place, time and causal dependencies of things from the things themselves, it requires language to designate, retain and impart these products of thought. This process of abstraction commencing in the human mind calls at once for language, and is carried on in and by it in exhaustless phases of growth. Speech is the supreme instrument of abstract thought, and all thought proper is abstract. Even the proper noun, though in the outset it may be merely an associative symbol, like the name of a dog, which gives a common token between the mas-

ter and his faithful attendant, is tending constantly
in the human mind to gain an abstract character, and so to become a common noun.   Even
nouns which remain proper nouns, as Daniel
Webster, do not, in the majority of cases, evoke
definite, sensible images, coming out as a person
in the panorama of a dream, but stand for a vague
knowledge of history and characteristics.   In this
they greatly differ from the concrete images which
occupy the consciousness of the brute.   The common noun, the adjective, the verb are all abstract ;
while adverbs, prepositions and conjunctions are so
wholly and flexibly abstract as to shift their meanings into the greatest variety of relations.   The
moment we wish to separate persons from a set of
concrete impressions which stand for them, to deal
with persons or things aside from their present relation to our senses, we must have language to
hold and to convey our analysis.   The present
must be distinguished from the past and the future ; the place we occupy from other places ; and
effects in our organism from those general effects
which we ascribe to an object when we are not
present.   This whole process is a breaking up of
the concrete, a separation in the mind of the floating facts of the senses or of the imagination, trans-
lating them into abstractions and reuniting them
in the supersensual relations of the reason.   Thus
one event becomes the cause, effect, condition of
another.   Such a transfer from the susceptibilities
to the thoughts, from the senses to the intuitions
and judgments, demands, as its indispensable con-

dition, language.   If rational powers are present,
they cannot miss language in their development ;
if they are not present, language, the instrument
of the rational process, cannot be taken up, no
matter how assiduously it is forced upon the attention.   The parrot's speech will remain " parrot-
like " to the end of the chapter.

Because with us abstract processes are always
playing about concrete, real and imaginative experiences, we find it very difficult to believe that it is
not thus with the brute.   This judgment is itself
an associative one.   Every consideration is against
the supposition.   The master is absent, the dog suf-
fers emotionally from his absence and follows his
foot-steps. A series of impressions succeed one another accompanied with appropriate action.   In the
absence of a friend, we also feel a vague sense of
want, but immediately turn it into a series of re-
flections and rational actions.   We are not driven on
as the dog by a series of images and sensuous impressions, which work their own way into our
muscles.   Times, distances, duties, dignity, all abstract considerations, overshadow and control our
action.

The young of animals adapt their motions to
spaces without recognizing them as spaces, and the
mature animal sensationally distinguishes between
things present and absent without abstracting those ,
relations from the facts expressed under them.   This
we may do in our idle, dreamy moods, but cannot
do when our attention is directed to the facts.   The
reason and the senses are coördinate with us, and

the facts contain, for one set of powers, relations ;
as certainly as they do, for the other set of powers,
sensible properties. No more can we deal with the
facts of the world without language, giving points
of fixation and transition to the rational process, as
do colors, flavors and sounds to the sensational
movement. The swallow poises itself in the wind,
or suddenly falls off before it, with a complete mastery of the mechanical problem ; the horse guides
his hind feet by impressions that have already left
the eyes ; yet here is organic construction acted on
directly by sensations—not reflection.

That the animal does not and cannot learn language, no matter how glibly he repeats it, is decisive proof that he fails of abstraction, the incipient
act of rational powers. That men always and
everywhere do create and use language proves as
decisively the presence in them of rational insight,
presiding over sensations, and making of them the
material of thought. The most concrete speech of
man, no matter how strongly this concrete character in rude languages may be insisted on, is full of
abstractions, expressed or implied. Indeed without
expressed or implied abstraction, language could
have little use, since it would be a needless reproduction of sensations. We are to remember also
that this absolute destitution of language proper
remains in the brute, notwithstanding the most protracted association with man, the most patient efforts to teach it him, and vocal powers that are
quite sufficient for the purpose. The wonderfully
trained dogs already referred to, whose performances

are fully given in Hamerton's Chapters on Animals, lost all their knowledge of written language on the death of their master. Those into whose hands they then fell could " get no performance out of them whatever." * This fact of language, so clearly indicative in itself of the faculties of animals and of men, is obscured in its force by weakness of analysis at two points. We do not distinguish between language as a natural expression of a concrete state or an associative symbol evoking such a state, and a system of signs, the instruments of a pure thought-process. We also persist in thinking that the same sense-images must, in all minds that consciously receive them, have the same power to evoke thought that they have with us. Thinking and dreaming are profoundly unlike, though human experience, taking in both phases, more or less modifies the one by the other.

We will now consider a very few of the more marked manifestations of associative life, applying to them the view here presented. It is quite immaterial whether we can or can not give a plausible explanation of them all. The most sagacious interpretation is not necessarily a correct one, and associations whose origin is very obscure to us may none the less be of a very simple character. It is not in the least surprising that the experience of alert animals, full of instinctive tendencies, should show some strange combinations, a sagacious good fortune often quite equal to the average efforts of rea-

* P. 253.

son. Perfectly blind forces, if given repeated trials, will yield curious relations, much more the lively discriminating senses of an animal. The dog, a sharp observer, yet having but little to observe, following its master like his shadow, and putting itself in sympathetic contact with him at many points, will sometimes reflect his states in a startling way, will take into its emotional consciousness the higher experience with a sudden disclosure, like that of clear images in a pool of water. The dog may even seem to catch from its master moral states, which are only a sensitive response to his censure or approval. It is a very inadequate notion of the associative life that would lead one to expect us to be able in each case to trace these lines of connection. We are not near enough to it. Nor can we even follow with certainty the silent links of reasoning which have led this or that man to his open conclusions.

We are, also, to remember that the stories which record the sagacity of animals are told with very little discrimination, and much exaggeration. They are likely to be deeply colored with human sentiment and human thought, simply because the narrator cannot conceive the naked facts without those implied thoughts and feelings as their causes. Very few men can separate the processes of reasoning which seem to be indicated by certain acts from the acts themselves, and so give these in an ungarnished tale. Not only are these facts very rarely recited by competent observers; they frequently 'fail to reach us first hand. Thus there are many stories of the same general character which are a common currency, circulating everywhere, and not often traceable with certainty to any specific case. The records of the sagacity of animals, therefore, need about the same amount of sifting as the myths and heroic traditions of a nation.

An orang-outang is credited with a sense of humor, because in the Zoölogical Gardens of London he acquired the habit of exciting this feeling in spectators by inverting his porringer, like a bonnet, over his head. This act, with the grimace and human caricature of the animal, provoked laughter. Assuredly the orang was sensible of the pleasure of his admirers, and would quickly learn the method of securing it. When Trip wags his tail because he is called a good dog, we need not infer that he has taken his first lesson in righteousness; nor need we regard an orang as a disciple of Rabelais, because he knows when people grin.

A power which, interpreted as rational discernment, would imply faculties of a high order is the sense of direction which belongs to many animals, and one which belongs to some of the lower as well as to the higher ones. The dog, cat, horse, ass, find their way to their old haunts through territory absolutely new to them, or which has been traveled over but once with little or no opportunity for observation. This subject received extended discussion and illustration in successive numbers of Nature a few years since. The conclusion was gathered up in these words : " The only out-come of this discussion has been to intensify the previous belief

in the existence of some unexplained faculty which
may provisionally be termed a sense of direction." *
Mr. Wallace, in the course of the discussion, urged,
as we think wisely, the view that animals are greatly
aided by the sense of smell in tracing a course
which they have once passed over ; this sense furnishing a series of impressions which can be used
by the animal as we use those of sight. Hamerton
says of himself, " I distinctly remember the odors
of every house that was familiar to me in boyhood,
and should recognize it at once." † There can be
no doubt that smell is a primary linear sense in animals.

That the nervous system through the senses is
capable of receiving in some undefined way without
judgment an impression of directions seems certain and necessary. Even in action at small distances this is called for. The shark will strike with
unerring certainty an object touching any part of
its body ; all hunting, as of insects by birds, involves the most immediate and exact discrimination of directions. This sense in a rudimentary
form must accompany every outward activity, and
must enlarge and confirm itself as the circle of effort expands. Even in man, rational estimates do
not wholly suspend this instinctive force of obscure
automatic impressions. At short distances in gym-
nastic exercises and games, this instinctive, organic
precision is a primary power, applied in a great variety of ways, and confirmed by the muscular train-

* Vol. viii. p. 282.　　† Chapters on Animals, p. 36.

ing which it none the less guides.   It also operates in us much more broadly, as in threading the streets of a city, or in settling directions in a forest.   Its frequently instinctive character is seen in the fact that one takes up, he knows not how, a false impression of directions in a strange place, and no reasoning process, not even the action of the senses, can correct it.   It endures with the most annoying obstinacy.   The more just and decided our ordinary impressions of direction, the more fixed these hallucinations when they have found entrance.   The sagacity of animals in finding their way is to be explained, we believe, by an undefined, automatic element, belonging to the original harmonizing power of the nervous system, and of which the impression just referred to is a remnant in man.   Even when we know the conditions operative in giving a false sense of direction, that knowledge does not serve to correct it, showing that it is not a matter of judgment merely.*

* Nor is a sense of direction hardly more strange than the sense of equilibrium which accompanies all our waking movements, and which leads us to maintain the body in an erect attitude, or its centre of gravity within its base, by so many, and so completely automatic adjustments.   In the most accomplished equilibrist, the requisite action still preserves its spontaneous character.   Nor are the sources of the stimuli which take part in equilibration less remarkable.   They are visceral impressions, tactile impressions, and labyrinthine impressions, or those of the semi-circular canals of the ear.   We have thus, as shown by Ferrier, in the apparatus of the ear an unexpected source of the most necessary stimuli in our ordinary movements.   A change of position in any of the three perpendicular planes of movement is at once automatically indicated to the muscular system and made operative through it.   The general disturbances of sea-sickness undoubtedly have something to do with a derangement of automatic stimuli pertaining to position.

The chimpanzee cracks nuts with a stone; the ossifrage breaks the shell of the tortoise or splits a bone by dropping it from a great height. The sagacity in these cases, like that which leads a cat to open a door by putting his paw upon the thumbpiece, may be easily arrived at by one or two fortunate associations. The tortoise, carried off hastily in flight and dropped by accident, would disclose the secret; while inheritance would transmit it. That a stone, by a lucky hap, should in one case be made an instrument, is less surprising than would be its confinement to a single use, if that use originated in reason. When the donkey feigns death to escape toil, or the fox to escape death, instead of its being the latest and trickiest device of thought, it is probably the earliest and stupidest tendency of instinct, innate in the bug in your path.

A writer in Nature, dwelling on the quick response which horses often make to signs of danger in the forest, or on picket-duty, or to the notes of war, in many instances surpassing their masters in discernment, sums up the significancy of these facts as " simply this. Horses think, horses reason, horses classify, horses remember." * That horses remember, and so classify automatically their experience in associative judgments, we readily believe, and that these processes, instituted by peculiar and alert senses, will surpass in results in a narrow field indolent reasoning, we also believe. But this very decision and superiority of the result we must

* Vol. viii. p. 78.

refer to its associative character, as we do the blind fright which horses so often exhibit, and which the least reason would correct. Jealousy in dogs, revenge in camels and in elephants, as unusually strong impulses, may lead them to protracted watchfulness, and so suddenly break out in an act of retaliation that may have all the appearance of a well-devised plot. Time plots for them, and they come in at the instant, and therein is the genius of anger.

Kirby and Spence narrate an instance of sagacity in a wasp, as given by Mr. Darwin. The wasp captured a fly nearly as large as itself. It cut off the head and abdomen, and then flew away with it. Finding itself still too much impeded, it alighted and sawed off the wings. " Could any process of ratiocination be more perfect?"* the authors inquire. They then proceed to instance a like fitting of cockroaches to the size of the hole into which the wasps wished to drag them. We are to bear in mind in these cases that the animals are working in the most direct line of their instincts, their constitutional, constructive skill. We must have one theory, not two. The wasp, the bee, the ant, the beetle, have constant occasion for measurements, definite sizes and shapes. Are these reached automatically or rationally? If we say the common results of their activity, involving size and position in so many particulars, are to be referred to a constitutional, constructive power, slightly modified by associations, then we have no occasion to take a

* Entomology, p. 562.

particular instance, make it striking by isolation, and refer it to reason. Such a method lacks all homogeneity. If these insects can do their ordinary work without weights and measures, they can do this as well.*

We cite one more case of sagacity given by a writer in Nature. A horse is eating from a nose-bag. A pouter-pigeon flies directly at his eyes and flaps his wings furiously. The horse jerks his head, flirts his oats, and the pigeon eats them. The writer closes, " I leave it to your readers to consider the train of thought that must have passed through the pigeon's brain before it adopted the clever method above narrated of stealing the horse's provender."† Nothing could be simpler than the explanation of this device of the pigeon. The horse from any cause jerks his head and a few oats are dropped. The pigeon eats them, flies up and occasions a second flirt. The association is immediately established and remains what it was at the outset, save that the pigeon becomes more bold and violent in its effort, having learned its success. The thought is precisely that, and no more, which leads a hen to hop on to a bar, and open its feed-trough by its own weight.

* That the action of this wasp is purely instinctive is seen by the following fact :

After bringing the caterpillar to her nest, the wasp always leaves it before the entrance and goes in to see if everything is in order within the cavity.

" During this absence of the wasp, Fabre removed her booty to some distance, forty times in succession. Forty times the wasp brought it back, but each time examined her nest afresh before she attempted to put her prey into it."—*Brehm's Thierleben*, vol. ix. p. 280.

† Vol. viii, p. 324.

Before this question can be settled, whether the mental action of brutes is rational or associative, we must distinguish much more clearly between the two than is generally done, and direct our inquiries and experiments with corresponding care. Most of the facts that are brought forward to prove a rational process may be freely admitted without in the least affecting the question. We confess a certain relief and pleasure in contemplating these vast stretches of consciousness in the animal kingdom with a law of activity distinctly lower than our own. This twilight region of mind bears with it none of the awe, solemnity and fearfulness of insight. Its dangers are narrow, its responsibilities are nothing, its pains are in an undertone and transient, its pleasures are clear and simple. No alarms from a far-off future, no cruel ambitions, no sombre duties darken the passing hour, nor scatter and waste the joys which a life just conscious of itself is gathering. If our dumb cousins, seedlings at the foot of the tree, receive less light, they also suffer fewer fears and feel gentler winds. We could wish for them either no more knowledge than we think them to have, or far more than they are thought to have.

CHAPTER VIII.

RATIONAL LIFE.

WE have now reached the highest grade of intelligence, that of rational life. It is not difficult to indicate its points of preëminence as contrasted with what lies below it ; but it is difficult to conceive in their integrity the narrow horizons of instinct and association, accustomed as we are to the broader vision of reason. Forms which are distinctly rendered by day-light, colors that are sharply distinguished at noon-tide, fade away and melt into one vague impression, one unanalyzed fact, as night comes on. The circle of the senses closes in around the traveler, and the bearings of objects on immediate safety and comfort occupy his entire attention. So animal, as contrasted with rational life, is crowded into a narrow experience, and busies itself with things in immediate contact with its senses.

The crowning distinction of rational life is that it is one of relations and not of things, of intellectual constructions and not of sensible data, one whose impulse is found in intuitions rather than in sensations. This truth is somewhat hidden from us by the fact that these relations, in themselves supersensible, yet lie between sensible things, that perceptions and sensations give the points of crystallization, the positions between which run the insensible lines of thought. Yet it cannot be regarded as a very difficult piece of analysis to separate things as objects of sensations from those relations between things which the ingenious, rational mind is constantly disclosing to itself. Take an extended, complicated and beautiful building. The most unilluminated eye can discern its substance: the eye of an architect, sustained in its research by the observation and skill of a lifetime, is needed in order to see its proportions, adaptations, relations of material, constructive and æsthetic features. Now these relations in which the edifice is rendered by the architect, and to which it owes its interest, are not directly visible, but only indirectly, by an accompanying rational process. The clown can see the page of Homer, he cannot translate it; he can see the walls of the building, he cannot discern the thought that has gone into its erection.

The analysis, then, is the separation of relations from the sensible qualities, one and all, of the things between which they lie. Thus the material of thought is secured, while its simply phenomenal conditions are left behind.

All these relations are given intuitively, that is, by an insight of the mind which transcends that of the eye or the ear or the tip of the fingers. They can only thus be given, since they are not sensible qualities in any the most subtile form. To these relations alone all logical processes pertain. Things simply as sensible facts cannot be argued about, cannot appear in premises, or re-appear in conclusions, cannot be made the material of propositions. Phenomenal qualities as phenomenal are declared to the mind through its sense-organs, abide in those organs, and cannot, for a moment, be gotten out of them. It is only when we add to sensations such notions as identity, equality, sameness, difference, that logical processes, thought-processes, find attachment.

This, then, is the thing to be shown, that relations, the discernment of which is the function of reason, and the discussion of which is the function of the understanding, constitute the primary material of human intelligence as contrasted with animal intelligence, of rational life as compared with associative life. The chief difficulty in this effort arises from the fact that associative life is in us united with rational life, and the two processes so blend with and sustain each other, that we cannot easily separate them in our conceptions. As the man more and more forgets the experiences of the child, so have we more and more left behind us those of the brute.

Let us in this effort at analysis and contrast take first the relation of space. We are not to discuss the origin of the notion; we are simply to deal with its relations as supersensible, that is, as not directly seen, felt, heard. We do not see

lengths or feel breadths, any more than we hear
distance.   The relations of length and breadth
are ideas which may or may not be present in connection with certain sensations.   Yet when they
are clearly, consciously present, they are so in, by
and for, the mind.

Take the animal : what are its mental relations
to space ?   They are those submerged, automatic
ones which belong to sensations, operating as physical stimuli.   Take the perceptions of the eye :
there are involved in them differences which are
due to the relations of space, due to things as near
by or far off, as in one position or in another.
These sensible differences, as in themselves modifications of stimuli, may operate directly on the nervous organization, and so secure a coördination of
action in reference to them ; or they may be used
by the mind as language, converted in clear thought
into relations, and then be made the conditions of
voluntary adaptations.   The first result is reached
by merely organic, instinctive life, the second by
rational life only.   It ought not to be difficult for
us to believe that these slight differences of organic
stimuli due to distances can be made directly, organically operative on accompanying action, for
this is precisely what takes place in us in the great
majority of cases.   The only difference between
the man and the animal in walking is, that the man
automatically adapts his movements to space,
having previously impressed its relations on the
mind and eye by voluntary and conscious effort,
while the animal yields to like impressions as the

data of a simple, primitive, organic dependence.
The difference between the two lies in the origin
of the coördination, not in its nature.   The
higher voluntary powers in man have assumed partial control over functions which remain purely
organic in the brute.   There is no more mystery
in the animal's fitting his action to spaces without
distinctly considering them than there is in man's
doing the same thing.   The apparently voluntary
movements of the animal are as automatically co-
ordinated to spaces as are its stages of digestion
to the length of the intestinal canal.   The signs,
then, of space relations may be directly operative
as simple, sensible facts, or they may be translated
into thought, and so become indirectly efficient
through the medium of consciousness.   The first
is the method of automatic life, the second of
rational life.   Thinking is a detached, self-sustain-
ing process, which is operative on organic connections through will.   Mere vision no more involves
necessarily the interpretation of the signs of vision
than it involves a knowledge of the Greek alphabet.
The very subtile way in which an organic process
will go on under the most obscure stimuli, and that,
too, when liable to interference from the will, is
seen in our management of our tongues in eating.
This organ is very active in the movement of the
food, and may be called on to shape the sounds of
speech in the midst of the process, yet it easily es-
capes the cutting and grinding of the jaws.   When
one, however, has actually bitten his tongue, and so
had his attention directed to it, its government be-

comes more difficult. The voluntary impulses
break in on the involuntary ones without being able
to take their place, and a second injury follows the
first. The tongue is suddenly found clumsy and
quite in the way.

The experience of animals, however, is greatly
narrowed by this their relation to space. None of
its relations affect them except as they are directly
presented in modifications of sensations, or of
images the counterparts of sensations. The absent
dog misses his home, but does not conceive it to
be in such a place, with such and such distances.
He may none the less be correctly brought under a
series of sensations and associations, and so be restored to it ; but the process is momentarily constructive under the senses as it proceeds, and is not
constructed under clear, mental relations before it
commences. Thus an animal may retrace its own
steps, no matter how long the journey, with no anticipation of its weariness. Men even, if the constructive imagination is feeble and the estimate of distances vague, retravel a road and recall its impressions only as they actually behold them. The space,
then, in which animals live is shut down to that of
the senses, with such trifling enlargements as visions
deeply impressed on the memory may give ; while
the impulses to movement are derived directly
from sensations or from associations. In man this
automatic life is broken up by the rational processes, and, by the abstract relations of space, he is
put in possession for purposes of thought and often
of action of large areas of his own country, of other

countries, of the world, of the Universe. He thus enspheres himself in the whole creation, and puts it in service and order in the ministrations of mind.

A second relation, with less conspicuous sensible traces than that of space, is that of time. The time of animals is emphatically the present. So far as they attach any action to particular times, they seem to do it by returning appetites or wants, by those sensible impressions which belong to the waning day and year, and which can be made the grounds of association and of instinct. When a squirrel prepares in Summer the food of Winter, we attribute the action chiefly to instinct; and doubtless correctly, since an instinct of this nature runs deep down into the animal kingdom. The insect deposits its eggs under conditions which will furnish food for the larvæ, though she can have no knowledge of them. The dog will bury a bone already gnawed, or food to which he has no occasion to return. Instinctive and organic action is the method by which animal life is usually led to provide for wants so remote as to make no immediate impression on the sensibilities. When a class of sensations attend on a particular period, these may become the basis of associative judgments, acting independently, or mingling with instincts. Thus cattle may return to their yard at the close of day, or birds seek a warmer climate as the Winter approaches. Thus, the present, in one way or another, is always the fulcrum on which rests the lever by which the future reaches and affects animal life.

How completely in man is all this altered. Time,
as an abstract relation, is constantly present to his
thoughts, and the larger share of his actions assume their form from a clear recognition of its
divisions, natural and artificial. The future is always with him controlling the present, and often a
very remote future. Indeed, by no one fact is the
intellectual progress of man from the animal to the
rational plane of life more clearly indicated than by
the length of the periods he takes into consideration in his daily conduct. It is difficult to induce
the savage to put forth exertions which provide for
wants beyond those of the hour, while the civilized
man is only too much disposed to forecast the
wants of remote years, and weigh down the present
with the work of providing for them. The periods
that science occupies itself with, backward and forward, are practically infinite, and its steps no more
weary traversing the stretches of time than in traveling the boundless areas of space. Philanthropy
and religion are habitually casting their entire hopes
of labor on the future.

The notion, or mental incentive, under which
these labors of mind and heart are chiefly undertaken is still more remarkable for its supersensible
character. Space and time have a sensible language, not directly, but indirectly ; but causes, the
idea of control, are inserted everywhere by the positive vigor of the reason. What could be more completely supersensible than this notion of forces, of
causes, which the mind brings forward as the necessary sub-structure of all things and events, all the

efforts of life. This is the first thoroughly productive movement of mind. The distances of space the periods of time, are suggestive under it, since the sensible changes through which they arise in the senses would have no significance, were it not for causation, did not a change of position involve a change of appearances. The mind cannot move at all among things without expressly or impliedly availing itself of this idea, since no relation among things can possibly declare itself to us otherwise than by this assumption of causation.

The mind inserts no such notion between images, establishes no such relations between its own conceptions, but it no sooner has to do with actual, physical phenomena than it obstinately insists on this supersensible term, and can do nothing without it. No illustration could be more complete of the constructive power of thought as dependent on the introduction of its own insight into relations. Thus, this last and most comprehensive explanation of things turns on a conception which has no direct hold on the senses, and one which we have no reason to believe ever enters the consciousness of a brute. The simple associations of memory, turning on the conjunctions of time, order the conscious life of the animal in its sequences. The philosophy that would reduce human thought to a like succession destroys itself, as a series of this nature can have no power of proof any more than the idle conjunction of things. When connections are null, their proof is nothing, for proof is a connection.

When we pass to moral and religious facts, the ideas which control belief and action are, if possible, still more supersensible. In morals the law is that of right, the power of obedience that of liberty, and on these two transcendent notions conduct and character are conditioned. The truths of religion, though scarcely more removed from sense-perceptions, are still wider in their range, still farther beyond the verifications of experience. None of the conclusions of morals or of religion can be verified off from their own bases. It is by an inner and not by an outer experience, that they justify themselves to an intellectual constitution, that includes them not among its sensations, but in its full intuitional and emotional forms. Music can not commend itself to the eye, nor can a spiritual fact to an unspiritual temper. We have thus in every rational activity of man invisible relations which furnish its law, and as these activities become more and more distinctively spiritual the remoteness and intangibility of these relations increase, till at length the human soul finds itself standing face to face with the Infinite, and shaping its life for immortality under the invisible motives of the spiritual world.

We are also to observe that the force of this distinction between the brute mind and the rational mind is not destroyed by denying the reference of such ideas as space, time, causation, liberty, to intuitive powers. These notions, if they are not granted as intuitions, must, at least a part of them, be accepted as generalizations, and thus there is brought out in another form the preëminence of the powers of the mind in abstraction, as opposed to associative action in the senses, the very point that we are emphasizing as the distinctive feature between the two intellectual phases. The empirical philosophy, much straitened by its method, is compelled to discard some of these ideas, but their very presence as unverified, illusory impressions is something remarkable, and is itself a striking difference between animal and rational life. We have no hint that any such far-off spiritual visitants as these visions of the Infinite and immortality ever make their way into brute consciousness, or disturb with a strange, spiritual power its sluggish movements.

This supremacy in the mind of man of supersensible relations, involving, at every step of their construction or use, abstraction, is farther brought out by language, the special instrument or organ of a rational process. We do not believe that this endless separation of relations from the sensible objects between which they lie, this gliding from point to point in thought by invisible threads of dependence, can be so much as entered on without that grasp by the mind of primitive connections regarded by us as intuitive ; but waiving this, and allowing a process of abstraction to be the source of these ideas, it is yet plain that abstraction, and it only, constitutes the peculiar controlling necessity for language, a necessity which only the human mind experiences. That that mind is practically dependent on language for its development is universally admitted.   Without it it sinks into something more allied to idiocy than to animalism — it aborts.

In speaking of this relation of language to rational powers, we shall do better to take language in its later than in its earlier stages ; because its true constructive power is more declared, though it is certainly not hidden in any stage of development. A language relatively complete is the product toward which the mind is pressing under its latent powers from the very outset.   What language ultimately accomplishes for thought, that it was as an incipient tendency which led the mind to lay hold of and develop it.   We cannot see the plant in the bud, yet it is there as an unfolding law.   Nor does this fact interfere with another fact which is often so presented as to obscure it.   Language in its origin may have in it a very large associative element, may be in part, like the cries of an animal, the direct expression of a concrete state, but this element is at most the nutriment of the germ, not the germ itself ; that germ is the process of abstraction requiring an abstract instrument for its development.

Take any cultivated speech, like the English. Consider its participles, its conjunctions, prepositions, adverbs.   How inconceivably numerous and subtle are the relations they indicate.   The whole constructive force of our language is in them, save that which is found in the similar abstractions of inflexion, position and implication. The sentence would fall to pieces as so many words were it not for these asserted and implied relations.   Ruder languages may indicate these relations in modified ways, or less completely ; yet, if they are capable of rational use, if they are language proper, these connections are in some way and to some degree in them ; otherwise, there is no transfer of thought. This interdependence of words is the supreme feature of language; its method is that which preëminently distinguishes one language from another, and that inter-dependence is made up of the most subtile possible abstractions, in some sense more subtile when merely suggested than when asserted. Take the preposition *in*, multiply as you will the instances of its use, and there will be found strikingly diverse colors in some of them, and obscure shades of difference in most of them. In the box, in the place, in the fire, in the mind, in the time, in society, in virtue of, in relation to, in connection with, in intention, in activity, in rest ; in these and a hundred like examples, we see that the first relation was one of space, variable in its very germ, and thence traveling with the most flexible suggestiveness into every region of thought. Obscure and abstract as these transitions are, the mind finds no difficulty in traversing them, because it is even more subtile than are they. Thought can scarcely move so quickly from the physical to the spiritual, from one relation to another, as to elude or even tax the mind in its pursuit. The same free movement belongs to all these particles of speech, blown about like the spores of intellectual life, in their passage from meaning to meaning. Verbs and adjectives are only a little less noteworthy. Verbs and adjectives are systematically abstractions. The action or the quality is separated from the thing to which it pertains, and from the other actions and qualities with which it is associated. Verbs and adjectives are not direct, concrete products of sensations, but these products in every stage of decomposition and reconstruction, of analysis and synthesis, of dissolving sense-connections and newly appearing mental ones. Neither do nouns, the roots of language, long remain the signs of specific things, but become common nouns, abstract nouns, adjectives and verbs. Taking to themselves some quality or relation, the product of analysis, they are led off by it into some specific duty. Not even the proper noun can get much use in language save as we wish to make it the centre of abstract conceptions, to speak of the person in reference to space, time and causation.

An intelligence that has to do with things through the senses simply finds no occasion for speech. So long as objects are present, they are the centres and sources of emotions ; and when they are absent, they drop from consciousness, or return to it only as a vision, operative on action like any other sensible fact. There can be no desire to speak about things, till the mind takes them up in abstract relations that require to be marked and transferred by designations. A brute certainly communicates its feelings, but these find expression as present facts or forces through natural effects, and are no more language than the babbling of brooks or the murmur of pines. Not an example can be given with any certainty under careful analysis of the transfer in language of an abstract idea from animal to animal. Natural signs cannot be language and remain natural signs, since that which makes them to be natural signs shows them to be the immediate products of organic forces, and not, therefore, the expression of a purely mental fact. Language, as the conventional expression of abstract relations, can arise only as the accompaniment of rational powers. Nor, if the theory of language be true that its roots are onomatopoetic signs, would its relation to our rational powers be in the least altered. The architect may use the stones in the street to erect his building. Language begins at once to depart from this basis, and is language by virtue of its departure. Doubtless the speech of savages has a relatively larger concrete element than that of cultivated nations, but if we add to words the relations involved in their exposition by the mind, if we restore to sounds their submerged as well as their visible supports in language, there is no human tongue that is not permeated with abstractions. Indeed, if it were not, it could be of no practical use beyond the cries of animals. Things that are present to the senses need not, any more than money before us, call for counters in reckoning. It is only as we wish to put things in a mental relation of some sort, that we have occasion to indicate them, and to retain our constructive points, as the architect traces his plan in the sand.

The mingling of natural signs, the immediate product of organic life, with the abstract signs of mental conceptions, and the constant passage of the former into the latter, serve to confuse the mind in searching for the true office and relations of language. It is the second, the abstract, element only that has any especial significance in speech. The rational mind cannot miss these visible footholds supplied by language to its invisible footsteps, and meet with any large development. Nor can the rational powers when set in action fail to push language through all its stages of development, till, in its thousands of relations, ten thousands of words, and hundreds of thousands of meanings, it becomes the counterpart of the manifold ways in which mind separates and recombines things.

Nor does it in the least alter the true intellectual character of the movement that it avails itself of onomatopoetic sounds. The lower always approaches the higher by one boundary, and the higher always finds its base-line along this margin. It is none the less for that reason the higher. The organic life lies just below the conscious life and sustains it. So far as intelligence—that is, conscious states—finds expression in natural sounds, it is associative intelligence; and only when it transcends them by a mastery of relations, and so starts out for the exploration of new realms and buds into fresh growth, does it become rational intelligence.

That this superior, rational insight must at once put the lower powers into a new position is evident. Organic life is different in man from what it is in the higher animals, though certainly on the whole not less complete.   To a full circle of purely animal functions it adds offices which belong to it in its peculiar dependencies on rational life.   Such are the powers of articulation in their complete form; the powers of song, and of musical perception as conditioned on the structure of the ear; the powers of expression in blushing, weeping, smiling, laughing, and in the facial play of features.   The organic life is also capable in man of profound modifications in tone, induced by the voluntary powers.   This is seen in what we term carriage and gait, the grace and decision of movement, in clearness and completeness of articulation, in the compass of the voice, and in the depths and strength of respiration.   The organic powers can thus assume a more perfect form, and be worked up to a higher performance.

The organic life in man is also made much more dependent on the conscious life for its development.   In the lower animals, and to a great degree in the higher ones, sensations are organically correlated with the appropriate motions, as in walking and flying.   In man like relations are largely the result of experience, the coördination is consciously and protractedly established.   If this adaptation of actions to distances was secured perfectly and unconsciously by man, that fact would serve to anticipate and check those rational estimates on which his later progress depends.   This constant, unconscious correction of our movements, as in walking,—an automatic action in us that has grown up with and out of a voluntary one—must be present to relieve the rational powers; but if our life is to remain flexible, and capable of redirection, there must be the use and insertion of purely intellectual processes. The two elements, organic and rational, must be maintained in mutual ministration. When any particular sensations and actions have been protractedly correlated, we shift the dependence with great difficulty. Thus, a carpenter holds a nail and drives it with no consciousness of directing the blow by the eye ; but let the light be diverted and the hand instantly becomes uncertain. He would learn the simplest act under these new conditions with great difficulty. The deaf are dumb not through any defect in the organs of articulation, but because, in losing the sense of sound, they have lost the impressions with which the action of the vocal organs is usually united. The wonderful muscular flexibility involved in the free use of the voice grows up with the conscious, auditory life. In the deaf, who have learned to talk in connection with lip-reading, an entirely new coördination has been established.

While the conscious life is thus ever working its way downward into the organic life, this still retains essentially its old limits, and most of its independent power. Instinctive action, on the other hand, the extension upward of organic action under peculiar constitutional stimuli, almost wholly disappears in man. These instincts, covering the space between purely organic and purely intellectual action, were only a provisional occupation of ground to be ultimately held by the higher power. They may be compared to the scaffolding by means of which the final structure is erected. Before reason is present in vigor, while feeble associative processes are slowly working their way among many embarrassments, this insufficient action of the mind needs to be supported by vigorous constitutional tendencies, by instincts. Putting the same fact under the form of development, the organic life acquires and transmits special functions, peculiar coordinations of decided advantage to their possessor ; but the conscious life, when it comes, occupies the same ground still more successfully, and so supersedes the instinct, crowding back the organic function into a narrower circle. Instinct in man is an insignificant factor, and belongs chiefly to the dawn of his life. Some, misled by a superficial resemblance, have likened the intuitions of man to instincts. The difference between them is very great. They both act with decision, it is true ; but the certainty of the instinct is that of a machine, working equally well in light and in darkness ; the certainty of an intuition that of the mind, moving in clear light.

The ground rescued by the reason from the organic action known as instinct, is chiefly occupied in man by skill and habit, and kept open to new introductions and modifications by a pervasive, conscious power. The coördinations of skill, as in the pianist, are established by voluntary effort, maintained in practice automatically, kept plastic, reshaped and improved by farther effort. Habit is a like result, reached with less carefulness and decision in the voluntary action. We rise into skill, while we often allow ourselves to sink into habits, to come under automatic tendencies unfavorable to our true power. Thus the unconscious life is constantly springing up to sustain the conscious life, and proffer to it its forces. The well-trained man acquires in action much of the certainty of instinct with none of its inflexibility. The organic life creeps upward as habit, and covers any ground that may be vacant between it and the rational life ; and the rational life pushes downward as skill, and claims for its own ends the powers that are necessary to sustain its voluntary life.

Associative life is also assigned a subordinate position by the preponderance of the rational impulse. When this is feeble, as in a savage, mental constructions are either those of empirical associations, or are greatly warped by them. Of these irrational, associative judgments, the innumerable superstitions of the lower races are an excellent example. They have been foisted on the mind by accidental conjunctions. When the thoughtful and voluntary life gains power, associations are determined in their own character by it, and henceforth minister to it. Impressions are not united fortuitously in memory, but by causes and reasons. The unanalyzed associations of experience no longer occupy the mind ; a vigorous intelligence rises up to use them, and set their limits in shaping them to its own purposes. Thus the associations of the artistic mind are themselves artistic; of the scientific mind scientific, as they are formed under a controlling attention to special relations.

Associative judgments bear also in man the same relation oftentimes to rational judgments, that habitual actions do to purely voluntary ones. Rational judgments that are frequently repeated become associative judgments, the conscious connection of insight being dropped. Thus a word of frequent use loses its figurative force, and becomes literal in a new meaning. It takes up directly by association an idea which it had before expressed only indirectly, through a discerned resemblance. The thousand associative judgments which now constitute in perception our sense of distance, position, form, are a good illustration of the office which association performs in a single sense, like that of vision. The mind is relieved by it of the necessity of traveling over familiar ground in full-formed judgments, and enabled to pass on directly to new labors. The associative process is thus to the rational process what involuntary is to voluntary action; what organic functions are to intelligent ones. It is the storehouse of knowledge, the condition of the accumulation of rational power. Observe how one threads the familiar streets of a city, retaining unbroken the connections of thought; and observe, also, how one hears familiar truths and customary words with slight attention, and yet is aroused at once by any new or strange or untrue utterance. The rational power, having constructed its associations, leaves to them ordinary action, and reserves itself for an occasion.

The lower life thus in every phase underlies the higher life, tends to push up into it and take its place, when this is feeble; or, when this is strong, readily gives way before it, and ministers to it. Man could do little or nothing as a rational being, could not his purposes and thoughts be passed over for execution to the associative and organic forces, which lie below them. These relations at once limit and enlarge, constitute and define our powers.

The lower development, as now presented, prepares the way for the higher, and when this is reached takes a position of service under it. This higher life, however, has its own germs, its own centres, and is in no sense the product of the powers below it. These are conditions to it, the pedestal on which it stands, but are not it. Thus development provides for a long delay in the appearance of reason, and yet for its rapid growth when it comes. The accumulations of life in each successive stage, as organic, instinctive and associative, self-sufficing as each one of these stages have been, are none the less all put at the disposal of reason, and are ready to unite with it in a yet higher unfolding. Thus the steps are each good, and all together, very good.

That the centres of each higher life are distinct, are seen in their very nature. Instinct, indeed, may be regarded as organic life unfolded in a new direction, shaping itself toward the more remote dependencies of its environment, but associative life has an absolutely new element in consciousness, and rational life in the intuitions. Each of them clusters about this new factor. This fact of a true increment is also disclosed in the fact that each succeeding term reacts most vigorously on previous ones. A simple development in a continuous line, an increased involution of identical forces, could hardly do this. The growth of intelligence as a whole is not one merely of accumulations, the thickening of an old stratum, but later terms give new results. Like the second centre or focus in an ellipse, reconstructing the entire figure, they call out new relations, and require a discussion of their own. Conscious powers supersede instinctive ones ; reason invades the lower life to reshape it under its own ends, and so declares itself, not an additive tendency, but a new and culminating government.

The same independence is also seen in the sudden way in which the rational movement proceeds when it has found inception. A nation, like the Greek or the English nation, will push over large spaces in an inconsiderable period ; or, which is more to the point, as there are many accidental and irrelevant considerations to retard national development, individuals will leave many boundaries and many grades of knowledge behind them in a life-time. Genius is not slow-paced evolution, but the sudden disclosure of surprising potentialities. The lowest races also, while capable in some instances of a collective movement that is astonishing, will, in favored individuals, pass over at once half or two-thirds of the ground that divides the lowest from the highest men.

Most evolutionists would put the native Australian well down toward the lower boundary of human intelligence ; and some of them would place him not far from midway between the highest animals and the highest men.*　Yet the children of Australians still on the plains, gathered up in the English government-schools, win equal rewards in scholarship with the children of Englishmen.　Dr. A. M. Henderson, long a resident of Melbourne, who stated this fact to me, put it even somewhat stronger.　As these awards of proficiency in the several schools are official, the statement is a simple one, and does not easily admit of mistake.†

Let any one make his selection among animals, and bend his whole strength to the effort, and see how considerable a part of this lower half of the division can be ‑traversed.　The relative ease of movement over all the interspaces of human intelligence, and the insuperable barriers which its boundaries present to those without them, show plainly that there is in man a new departure under its own conditions.

That the progress of nations and races as contrasted with that of individuals is slow, or that when it becomes rapid through vigorous external influences, as in the case of the Hawaiians, it is liable to be in a measure superficial and illusory,

---

* Cosmic Philosophy, vol. ii. p. 294.

† An official report before me says of one of these schools at Lake Wellington: "The examinations by the government-school inspector have been very good again, and the whole 5th class have passed the standard examination, and received their certificates." A written report of the same school, by James Holland, says: "The children of this school have again passed a most creditable examination.　They display a really very remarkable amount of intelligence and quickness."

are facts that do not materially affect our argument. We are discussing the potentiality of the human type, and every individual represents that type; Toussaint L'Ouverture as truly as his lowest fellow-countryman. The laws which control social development bring in new principles beyond those of the potentiality of the type, the individual. They introduce choice, and ethical actions and reactions in a complicated and extended form.

The intuitions which are to us the organizing forces of spiritual life are referred by evolutionists conjointly to experience and inheritance. The chief gain of the introduction of this new element of heredity is thought to be that it sufficiently explains the sense of necessity and certainty which often accompanies these intuitions, as for example the axioms which pertain to space, the notion of causation, and of moral obligation. " The necessity of a belief and its experimental origin," says this philosophy, " are but two sides of the same fundamental fact." * " The universality and the necessity of unconditional propositions, whether relating to space-relations, or to any other relations whatsoever, must inevitably result from the absolute uniformity in the organic registration of experiences, and does not therefore involve any *a priori* element." † The transfer by inheritance of this perfect unity of organic impression is assumed as the true explanation of the depths of the rut into which the movements of mind have fallen in

* Cosmic Philosophy, vol. i. p. 149.　† Ibid. vol. i. p. 101.

these directions. The new doctrine seems to us more remarkable for its tacit confession of failure in previous presentations from the same sources than for the skill with which it makes good the acknowledged deficiency.

The thing to be explained is the depth of certain clear convictions, for example, that two straight lines cannot enclose a space. This certainty is referred to uniform experience and transmitted impressions. A difficulty which would strike any mind at once in this theory is that many of these necessary truths, indeed the most of them, are removed in their statement and definite perception from ordinary, undeveloped intelligence, and would, therefore, have had no opportunity to accumulate conviction. The conceptions and curves of mathematics, the axioms of logic, the highest statements of ethics, have no repeated statement in the general current of human experience, and could have gained no confirmation in this way. We are to remember, moreover, that it is the clear conscious hold of these truths on the mind that is to be explained, not an unconscious, automatic one. Let us return in thought to the first experience in the history of intelligence in which any one of these convictions came out in its true force. If the truth, being then present as a truth by virtue of its own inherent power, did seem to involve an *a priori* element, that conviction might indeed have been transmitted, if it were a proper subject of heredity; but could not itself be explained by it. Could it be explained by the transmission of some-

thing other than itself, prior to itself, and the fore-
shadowing of itself? We think not. These convictions are living convictions, insights, not organic
sequences ; hence the transmission of any automatic connections inferior to them could not, by
simple repetition, be transmuted into them. Transmission alters nothing, introduces no new element.
It may confirm a line of sequence, but it cannot
transform it into an insight. Our most complete
skill brings no new vision of relations. Hence, as
our purpose is to explain an intellectual conviction,
a true insight of mind, we are not helped by a
theory which refers it to anything lower than itself, no matter how often that inferior relation may
have been repeated. Repetition issues in habit,
not in knowledge. The inquiry still returns, How
came the mind clearly, consciously to reach these
experiences? No amount of previous automatic
action can answer this question.

This theory lays hold of a single fact, overlooks
its dependencies, exaggerates it, and then assigns
it an impossible work. The conscious, voluntary
conditions of any particular series of actions may
indeed pass away, and the movement remain only
the more certain ; formal judgments may sink into
associative ones, and these be not less serviceable ;
but this class of facts does not disprove higher
powers, nor dispose of them, but only shows their
necessity. They are instances of the way in which
the higher as higher reacts on and rules the lower.
They furnish no analogy by which to explain those
clear intuitions which often spring up at once in

the mind. These secondary facts which have given rise to the theory, when seen in their true relations, are found quite alien to the higher insights of the mind, and, in the phenomena which they do explain, to involve the previous action of superior powers.

This opens the way to a farther answer ; the theory evolves the lower out of the higher, not the higher out of the lower, and so reverses the true sequence of evolution. The lower prepares the way for the higher, and then the higher, present as a true increment, reacts on the lower, and thoroughly subordinates it to itself. The strict, narrow theory of evolution cannot neglect this order of sequence, though it refuses to recognize a real increment. But the view of intuitions under consideration, having its attention exclusively occupied by this reaction of the higher on the lower, struggles to invert their entire dependence, and put associative experience before instinct, and rational experience before intuitions. The bird is thought to accumulate knowledge, and transmit it as an instinct of migration ; the mind of man to frame in experience an obscure precept of morality, and to transmit it as a luminous principle. Thus because the higher does attach itself to the lower and modify it, experience softening instincts and confirming intuitions, this fact is laid hold of as typical, and the inferior development is made to follow bodily from the superior one. Experience as a whole is a higher term in evolution than instinct, and must have its support. Instinct can no more be made to depend primarily on experience, than organic function could be made, by like reasoning, to follow after instinct. Equally futile is it to liken the certainty and necessity of intuitional truths to the force of habit, and then derive them from the repetitions of experience. The error here is double. The intuition is first degraded to a semi-organic connection, and then made to follow intellectual processes as lower than they. The intuition is not lower, but higher than the judgments of experience; but if it *be* lower than they are, then it cannot be referred in sequence to them. This is to build from the top downward; and the only analogue on which this great constructive error rests is found in the reactions here and there of the higher on the lower. Study our intuitions carefully and candidly, and we shall see that they cannot be identified with the transmitted ties of instinct. Or so identify them, if we will, with such organic dependencies, and we shall then see that as lower products in our constitution they cannot be made to follow as a whole from higher, conscious powers. The secondary modifications of instinct which arise under experience can assume no such constructive force as belongs to the intuitions, shaping our entire intellectual development.

Our last difficulty with this derivation is that it finds no support in the laws of descent. Intuitions are not transmissible material. There are three tendencies in descent whose relations to each other are not yet well defined; the primary law of transmission, by which the characteristics of the parent reappear in the offspring; the law of atavism, by which tendencies long since left behind suddenly revive; and the law of variation, by which undefined and also decisive differences are constantly arising, referred, without, however, any insight into actual dependencies, to the varying circumstances of a changeable environment. We are now alone interested in the first of these three terms, that of immediate inheritance. This law plainly rests on the organic life. It is associated with life from its very beginning, and is as constant a part of it as any one of its potentialities. This seems to us to be in every grade of intelligence its exclusive basis. Spiritual powers are not passed by inheritance, aside from their dependence on physical ones, Organic functions under each specific type are of course carried over habitually; this is a fundamental law in life. Though unexplained varieties may arise in descent, the law begins immediately to lay hold of the increment, and control it with much the same force with which it governs the ninety-nine parts of customary constitution. Though the law of inheritance relaxes enough in varieties to secure conditions of progress, it returns immediately to its steadfastness, and so holds the ground gained. Instincts as primarily organic are also transmitted in full vigor. The experience which attaches itself so directly to an instinct as to incorporate itself with it, like that which leads some birds, as the cliff-swallows, to modify their methods of nesting, also passes by descent. In the same way the acquired habits of dogs, that rest on any peculiar organic power or tendency are transmissible. Diseases which work themselves into organic structure are often inherited, while the results of accidents, essentially alien to organic tendency, make no impression on offspring. In man, vigorous, functional development that has been secured in part by voluntary effort may impart vigor to posterity, while that skill which lies in the mastery of muscles, having no organic relation to one office more than to another, but being principally dependent on the voluntary life, is not transferred. Yet, as all vigorous effort and active thought may increase functional force, it is quite possible for them, when ordered in a healthy way, to reappear in children as organic strength.

On the other hand, the more conscious and voluntary our acquisitions are, the less do they pass by inheritance. Skill, associative judgments, rational judgments, knowledge, character, moral purpose, are personal terms, transferred, if transferred at all, by the intellectual law of influence. They are possessions held by the mind, and subject to its conditions. Galton has plainly shown, by a large generalization from many examples, that marked intellectual ability in one member of a family is followed, as a rule, by some corresponding ability in other members. Yet, as this talent often arises suddenly, is very waveringly transmitted at the outset, and is almost always dissipated in two or three generations, these facts seem to be in entire harmony with the results we have a right to expect from simple, organic inheritance, and intellectual transfer, each under its own law. Unusual talent implies in some directions unusual organic vigor and fineness of nervous structure. These may well pass from father to child, and, without conditioning the intellectual character of the child on purely physical causes, may yet give him superior instruments of life. The station also and opportunities won by the father accrue unmistakably to the benefit of the son, and prepare for him an open, prosperous way. The instruction and influence of the father will usually lie in the same direction. It would, therefore, be very surprising, if facts did not disclose these combined influences working in behalf of the transfer of intellectual power. These tendencies of inheritance have been especially conspicuous in public men, statesmen and jurists. But success in public life calls for a strong physical development, while the position of the parent may give very unusual advantages to the son in a similar career.

Genius is far less transmissible than talent. The reason is obvious; it is less dependent on organic conditions and on culture. Health and study do less for it. Poets and artists are not born of poets and artists, because their powers are of so purely a spiritual character, and so much beyond the range of acquisition. Musicians have in some instances clustered together in lines of descent, but music involves a peculiar physical organization, and one that may be profoundly affected by practice. Moreover, this talent, in its moderate forms, is very dependent on cultivation.

In the drama, composition and representation
imply very different powers.   The first is more
purely intellectual; the second depends on a mercurial, impressible temperament, and vigorous,
flexible, physical powers.   Shakespeare was but an
indifferent actor.   The great dramatists die and
leave no heirs ; while the descendants of a Kemble
or a Kean may long tread the stage.

Intellectual transmission is primarily conditioned on the conscious and voluntary life, and only
indirectly on heredity.   The first terms of purely
spiritual powers, while greatly modified in their unfolding by organic conditions, remain first terms,
unexplained by any law of physical descent.   We
can no more dispense with original differences than
we can with the force of surrounding circumstances
and physical constitution.   Intellectual powers are
as supersensible in their dependence backward as
they are in their own nature, and in their development forward.   A rigorous law of physical descent
is only another assertion of the supremacy of matter
over mind, and is certainly not sustained by the
observation of daily life.   Almost every family will
bring some contradiction to it ; while nothing is
more marked than the sudden, volcanic way in
which men of intellectual and spiritual genius are
thrust up; or than the very limited traces they leave
behind them in their posterity.   There is indeed a
moral preparation for them, and a moral sequence
to them in society, but among genital forces they
stand alone.

If we apply this view of descent to the theory

under discussion, we shall see that our intuitions, as our very highest acts of intelligence, are least of all transferable by inheritance. The great geometrician, whose insights seem almost to create the laws which he discusses in many and remote relations, neither gets nor gives his treasures of knowledge by descent. The moralist or the reformer, who puts new constructions on social life, is as independent of ancestors as of the conventional sentiment that rules around him, and passes over his possessions only to those children of wisdom that can accept them. Not till we have greatly degraded our spiritual nature, can we turn its treasuries into blood currents. " Faith melteth into the blood " not directly but indirectly, by spiritual transfer and by secondary physical connections. Physical powers shall at length fall under the control of our spiritual nature with a fulness we have not dreamed of ; but only as it shall first come completely under its own law, and from its own position set up those just reactions in which the inferior puts itself in ministration to the superior.

If the growth and grades of intelligence are at all such in the animal kingdom as we have now presented them, there is a steady evolution of powers, but one sustained by slight and by decisive increments, and driven forward in definite lines. This we believe to be the true statement of the case, that the organic world is an evolution, but one whose first terms by no means contain its last ones, nor one which sinks into a purely automatic movement. That kingdom as a whole is a true growth, which bends in passing all forces to its uses, but itself, under its own law, enlarges and multiplies its offices as it proceeds. All that sustains strict physical evolution sustains this view of the world, and equally all that, transcending simple evolution, looks to constructive and specific powers, and the enlargement of resources in the stages of growth.

Aside from the innumerable minor increments that attend on all variations—variations which we cannot express in "terms of matter and motion," and must admit, therefore, at least provisionally, as true increments—we have a decided increment in the progress toward intelligence in the introduction of a nervous system, also manifest increments in the rise and stages of development of each special sense, and a still more decisive one in the dim dawn of consciousness, that first thin ray, the precursor of all intellectual light. Memory, also, something far more than the repetition of previous experiences, for these had been repeated from the very beginning without it, was, when it appeared, a new constructive power. By it were accumulated and bound together, as in an experience, those associative judgments which prepared the way for, and were to be slowly displaced by, the latest and largest increment, that of the insight of reason. No addition rested more directly on all that had gone before it than this of intuitions, and yet none brought with it such new life, and so large a modification of previous conditions, as the rational insight into those relations by which intelligence, proposing and pursuing ends, lays hold of physical forces as instruments provided to its hand.

A complete change in the plane of life speedily arose from it. Not only did the intellectual elements hidden from the eye in consciousness, and playing hitherto a subordinate purpose amid physical forces, at once gain ground, the line of development no longer rested with the individual on physical descent, but was transferred to the race in spiritual progress. It matters little, in the progress of animal life, whether the numbers contained in species are large or small, save as increasing the chances of variation, and as giving the conditions of natural selection. The steps of growth are physical, and, with the exception of those directly involved in a new variety, the species as a whole contribute nothing to it, but rather embarrass it. Herds among animals bring safety, scarcely anything more. Families among insects may minister to development, but it is instinctive rather than intellectual development. With man everything is altered. The seat of growth has been transferred to the mind, and the plane—rather than the line—of development has passed over to the race. The individual by himself is insignificant, an inferior animal ; united with his fellows, he is the receptive centre of powers radiating in from all directions— from nature below him, from the innumerable race of men around and behind him, and from the spiritual world above him.

Intelligence is unfolded under the action and reaction of many minds, the concurrent efforts of many persons; while the field of morality is social action, and its office the fit construction of these reciprocal relations. Our rational nature, then, can find development only in society ; thence comes its incentives and its aids to activity, and thither it returns its own gains. Here reign the spiritual laws of conduct and character. As a result of this development transferred to the race, the range of the individual is immensely increased, and is made practically infinite. All thought feeds his thought, all emotion flows in on his heart, and swells the stream of his life. Yet these immeasurable gifts are honestly his, and paid back in full with his gifts. As no limit can be set to the race in the variety, fecundity, and mobility of its intelligence, so no limit comes to the individual who is once engrafted into this stock, who holds by this trunk, and buds and blossoms among its branches. No more complete transfer of activity, without the loss of previous conditions, can well be made than this by which the individual is taken into the race, and finds his growth one with it. Life is first a physical hierarchy with innumerable gradations and ministrations ; but so finished, it makes way at once for a new spiritual kingdom, as cities spring up on some rich bottom-land, under the bright sun, amid the beautiful landscape. Surging seas, drifting floods, ploughing glaciers, lifting lands, sinking shore-lines, in all their processes of construction,— grinding, distributing, and recombining—no more directly prepare the way for vegetable life than this in turn ministers to animal life, and than this, working its way upward through the twilight of consciousness into the full dawn of intelligence, gives itself to spiritual functions in man.

If the lower, in its physical unfolding, furnishes the conditions of the higher, not less does the higher, through the forecast of a Presiding Intelligence, and the expansion of a rational purpose, include and expound the lower. If efficient causes explain the movement in its forces, so do final causes interpret it in its directions. It is interlaced upward and downward, backward and forward, by the two conjointly, and thus becomes complete by them both in its relation to the human mind.

On this canvas, so painstakingly prepared, laid in with such and so many colors, at last there comes forth a spiritual vision in ample and beautiful detail. Not to understand every part of it is to understand no part of it; not to perceive its consummation in man is to miss its stages of growth.

CHAPTER IX.

THE SUPREME REASON.

WHILE one class of philosophers deny to the notion of the infinite any intelligible basis, and so escape all discussion concerning the Infinite Reason save this first destructive one, another class transform in a very unintelligible and unwarrantable way all the conceptions to which this adjective is applied, and fall into the worse fault of making that which they admit inadmissible. Thus, because God is infinite, some are ready to deny to his action ordinary relations to space and time, and to regard these and the kindred categories of the reason as quite inapplicable to him. Thus, instead of remaining the Supreme Reason, the centre of light, he becomes a kind of Unreason, about which all darkness gathers. To deny these first conditions of knowledge and power to the divine attributes is not to enlarge them, but to make them perfectly unintelligible; is not to remove their limits, but to work in their very substance such changes as to make of them contradictions and nullities. Reason is one in nature, whether finite or infinite. The noun retains its definition, and the adjective gives it that extension of which this definition is capable. Infinite time is still time, with the limits which belong to any one finite period removed. Infinite space and infinite power are space and power, with all special restrictions shaken off. Infinite space does not become infinite time, nor infinite power infinite wisdom, but each remains to be understood as before in its own nature. Infinite intelligence or perfect intelligence is not something other than intelligence, but intelligence in its fullest, largest form. If the adjective breaks in on the noun, the thing designated does not pass to its perfect state, but begins to disappear altogether. Omnipotence that does not include all finite power under its own form is not omnipotent; nor is that omniscience which is not coëxtensive with the range of knowledge as knowledge. Omnipresence that should have no reference to space would become an unmeaning word.

So the Supreme Reason remains throughout, subject to the intrinsic laws of reason, to its primary categories. Space, time, causation are not of the nature of bounds or restrictions put upon rational action, they are those interior conditions which define it as rational. We at once, therefore, reject the idea that the knowledge and activities of God sustain any other relation to time, or to any of the categories of reason, than those known to us as rational; or that his power and intelligence become some wholly new and incomprehensible thing by being infinite. Finite power may be largely potential, and infinite power must be potential. The Infinite, by every act of definite realization passes its product of expressed power, how great soever that product may be, over into the finite. The Universe, whatever its dimensions, is as thoroughly finite as every one of its parts. The Infinite in power is the noumenon which we put back of its phenomena collectively taken. In the same way intelligence includes a large potential element. We know not only what is present to our thoughts, but all things which we can at pleasure recall to them. Infinite knowledge has its element of potentiality as well as finite knowledge. Knowledge *in posse* is as real, as effective, and as certain a term in reason as knowledge *in esse*, and the latter cannot, therefore, in the Supreme Reason exclude the former as in some way less perfect than itself. The two are more perfect than either term by itself, and put knowledge in definite relation to its primary categories of time, space, causation. To deny potentiality to knowledge is to destroy movement, and to break in on its real nature. It is as if we should say that infinite time cannot be dealt with by moments, nor infinite space be thought to contain finite measurements.

The things momentarily known by God can no more be infinite than the things momentarily done by him, since the two are the counterparts of each other. In the very knowing as in the very doing, the infinite potentiality passes into a finite fulfilment, comes under the categories of reason. The knowing like the doing of God can take on the

notion of the infinite only in such way as is consistent with its rational nature; its perfection and
infinity must, therefore, include the two elements,
the potential and the actual, as all movement, all
unfolding, all reason arise in the passage from the
one to the other.   On any other supposition the
unity and parallelism between the knowing and
doing of God, between the creative thought and
the Universe would be lost.   The actual manifestations of wisdom and-power go hand in hand, the
intelligence of God and the power of God are co-
ordinate terms in creation.   That the Universe in
its unfolding from era to era is the conscious
thought of God, the line of activity along which
his conceptions gather, through which his intellectual life is realized, uttered, made conscious to
himself and visible to us, seems just as certain as
it is that this alone is the one broad ocean of physical forces which is fed from his potentiality.   The
unity and parallelism of his activities are the counterparts of the unity and parallelism of his works.

At all events, this is the only way in which we
can know the knowledge of God, the only way in
which it is capable of being known, the way in
which it can be truly and justly known. The whole
movement has this sufficient confirmation that reason answers to reason in it, and knowledge yields
itself to knowledge; and there can be no more radical principle of proof than this.

But what are the differentiæ of Supreme Intelligence as contrasted with finite intelligence? This
question involves the further question, What are the

limitations of knowledge that are put upon us by our finiteness? That all our knowledge is not immediately conscious knowledge, knowledge ever before the mind in its steadfast gaze, is not such a restriction, but a rational incident to that flow of intellectual life which is itself the glory of life, and of which time is the abiding category. Change in consciousness is motion in the intellectual world as opposed to rest, life as opposed to death. It is itself a perfection involving all other perfections, strength, sympathy, righteousness. To insist that infinite knowledge is stationary, inert knowledge, is to degrade, not to exalt, it; to destroy, not to enlarge, spiritual being. Such a view overlooks the relation between the finite and the Infinite, the one in perpetual flow from and return to the other. As the present moment is the one only available point of eternity, that in which and by which alone the whole conception expresses itself, so is the existing Universe in each transitional stage that through which Infinite wisdom and power take their way, the point at which they dismiss the potential, pass into the actual, and accept the rational conditions of evolution. This conception of God brings us close to the very facts of the Universe, and makes them our momentary conditions of contact with him.

A first restriction incident to finite intelligence is its limited perception, its narrow knowledge of facts. Infinite Intelligence evokes all facts out of the light of its own creative thought, and so holds them all in perfect oversight. A second restriction is the weakness of the memory. Facts once known escape from us again, and perceptions and impressions flow through the mind like a river, rather than spread out in it like a lake. The Infinite Consciousness holds all facts in its horizon, and covers them like the overarching heavens. If, however, time, as we believe it to be, is an inwrought category of reason, which reason evolves in its first activities, God no more loses sight of the past, present and future than do we. These distinctions abide in the very nature of his thought, and so enter our minds because they are the eternal framework of reason. The past fact is past to God as decisively as to us. Any other view enthrones chaos and night again in place of the eternal light of reason. Complete perception gives the entire present, perfect memory the entire past, and unrestricted insight the future.

The third limitation of the mind of man is that it only slowly, and with much difficulty, traces the relations of ideas to each other, and the dependence of causes and effects on each other. Our ratiocinations are the tedious travel of the mind from place to place in the intellectual world, are at once our weakness and our strength, our pain and our pleasure. We have a narrow circle of self-evident truths, intuitions, and all farther truths are gotten laboriously in connection with them. The process of reasoning, as a necessity arising from the weakness of insight, belongs to finite intelligence, is constantly pushed aside even with us by intuition, and must wholly disappear before the complete sweep of the all-seeing eye, the range of the Supreme Reason, whose radius of vision lies athwart the physical and the spiritual Universe in their utmost compass. The substitution of intuition for ratiocination is not a change of relations, but of the rapidity with which they are seen. The paths of thought are the same, they are only traversed more quickly. Intuition moves instantly to the journey's end, while reasoning moves warily, wearily, and often halts in its exhaustion. God does not reason, he sees; and sees from the beginning to the end.

This fact of insight does not, however, create causal sequences where there are no such sequences. It does not call out conclusions where there are no premises on which they can rest. The logical coherences of thought and physical causation still remain the lines of rational movement and of complete insight. The future is known so far as it lies open to intuition in its overruling principles, but is not known in its spontaneity and freedom beyond the qualified knowledge which these relations imply. These creative energies retain their nature just as certainly under the divine insight that orders their conditions as under human scrutiny. The points of relatively independent power in his work put upon the Divine Nature no limitations, but may best of all express his attributes. We proceed in all this on our fundamental truth, that reason is coherent throughout; and for it to abolish in its own name at any point its fundamental distinctions, by way of magnifying in some unknown way some unknown factors of power, is suicidal, is the resignation in its own name of its own supremacy. This is to say to Chaos, Thou art the mother of all things, to thee let our thoughts make haste to return.

A fourth limitation of human intelligence is found in the comparatively few things which it can at the same time twist into the thread of its thought. A half-dozen objects may occupy the attention, and though these may representatively involve many others, yet the exclusion always far outweighs the inclusion. It is with the mind as with the eye; its horizon is not very far off, and the things within it are held with much obscurity. Hence the line of actual experience includes, even in the most comprehensive minds, but a small parts of the facts which are pressing in upon it, and leaves an infinitely larger number, many of which might be very pertinent to its purposes, wholly beyond its survey.

The Supreme Reason gathers its included data from the entire compass of facts, as fibres from every portion of the distaff pass into thread till each shed of material is consumed, or as the nerves of sensation in man come in from every part of the physical periphery, and centre in the brain.

The conscious life of God is thus complete and commensurate with the creation. Perfect perception, perfect memory, absolute insight, unexhausted attention, make the knowledge of God the counterpart of those manifold processes which are brought together in the Universe, and in the Universe pushed forward in ever enlarging development. The consciousness of God is thus the transition term between the finite and the Infinite. These rational processes in progress about us are the very data from which we infer the Divine Mind, and equally, therefore, must infer the *form and expression* of Divine Intelligence.

We do not, of course, say that this view is without difficulties, without darkness on all sides ; we only say that it seems to us most modestly, yet most firmly, to hold fast as real what we seem to know, and to refuse to surrender it on reasons drawn from what we do not know, and destructive to the very process of knowing. It expounds the abstract by the concrete, and keeps near in its expositions to the actual starting points of knowledge. It takes its station with the light, the feeble light, if you please, of reason, and holds aloof therewith the enveloping darkness, eager to swallow all up again. It is faithful to its first terms of thought, and yet waits for their enlargement. It will not, with the Positive Philosophy, say that sensation is the compass of knowledge, nor yet in bold idealism allow its conceptions to slip from a constant confirmation by facts. Things and thoughts are put in perpetual interaction and on mutual interpretation.

It takes little heed, therefore, of objections which, like Mansel's riddles of the infinite, arise from the verbal expansion of a transcendental conception ; or of objections which rest exclusively on the narrow, crass experience of the physicist. Of the latter order is the difficulty already alluded to, that mind is united to matter only through a nervous system, therefore that the consciousness of God, if real, must somewhere find its cerebrum, cerebellum and spinal cord. In our finiteness we are conditioned in power and at the same time granted power by an ability to touch and rule the physical world—by this very fact that certain resources of energy and storehouses of force are put at our disposal in the body. These become our capital, our first investment in actual life. Such a relation is incident to the fact that we come into a world complete in itself, realized in all its forces and tendencies long ago, and that our bodies are made our points of attachment to it. When we reason to the Infinite, these relations of secondary dependence, from the very nature of the argument, are impertinent, and must be dropped. Not only finiteness, but its necessary incidents disappear. The argument is rendered irrational and suicidal by any other method ; as much so as to say, we are finite, all things are finite, therefore the Infinite is finite. If we are to reason to the Infinite, we must grant the Infinite as a conception, and it is a denial of this conception to say that God must have a brain, arguing it from experience ; that his thought and power, like those of man, must be conditioned on a coëxtensive relation of matter and mind. This is to destroy the Infinite by dividing the Universe between two elements, the physical and the mental ; and is to give to matter more than its moiety of power, since it settles for mind the conditions and limits of activity, both as being that in union with which alone mind can be, and as being that in which and by which and under which alone mind can work. Reason has a far more profound penetration into the antecedent conditions of its problems than this assertion implies. Such difficulties are begotten as creeping larvæ of the empirical philosophy. Yet even the clear, bold mind of Martineau seems to find some force in them, and he is ready to start suggestions as to the possible brain of God. If we go stumbling about with the plumb lines of experience in this way, the rectitude of the Universe will be a very narrow, relative affair of our own.

What is the relation of the Supreme Reason to matter, to life, to mind? Can we say anything intelligibly about these relations? Is there any valuable purpose subserved by outlying theories on these points? If we answer the second question in the affirmative, we shall answer the third in the same way. Coherent thoughts on these topics, though they may be no more to the mental eye than are shreds of clouds in the sky to physical vision, may yet keep these spiritual fields open to the mind, hint to us their true nature and depth, make visible the otherwise invisible passage of light through them, and so retain us in an attitude to receive knowledge when knowledge shall come to us. The trouble is that our narrow, physical experiences tend to obscure the whole topic, to make us short-sighted, and to close the way to insight with doubts that have no deeper ground than the narrow range of the senses. Thus we repeat in philosophy the great error of morals, in allowing our lower nature to give standards to our higher nature. We believe it great gain to occupy this ground of ultimate relations with conceptions that spring from our rational intuitions, if only to drive back and hold back those grosser and narrower ones, that, with no rightful ownership, come in in the name of science to preempt the spiritual realm. The analogues, the suggestions, the types of interpretation with which we approach the Supreme Reason must be taken from reason, from mind and not from matter, from philosophy not from science. Any walls which we shall place on the earth, and build up to Heaven, will be Babel walls, occasions of confusion and overthrow.

We find in matter, and operative upon it, certain fixed forces. These are the true noumena which the mind, by an insight and necessity of its own, puts back of all phenomena, converting these into the effects of which those are the causes. These forces have that definite adaptation to each other, and that mathematical precision which are the crowning marks of intelligence. They bear as distinctly as anything can bear these two indications of reason, a supersensible source and exact relationship to each other. The first is emphasized by the way in which matter breaks up into ultimate atoms, which are only ultimate centres of activity; and the second by the way in which each of these forms of activity stands correlated with other activities, and is expressed through them. There is thus to matter no undissolved nucleus, and no independent quality. These activities, so supersensible in being, so comprehensive and exact in relationship, we refer, therefore, directly to the

Supreme Productive Reason. Against this view their steadfastness may cause the thought to militate. But reason may be steadfast, in its first principles is steadfast, as steadfast as mathematical truth.

In living things we find these forces curiously combined, wonderfully watched over, varied in their manifestations, compacted into distinct types; and these types, with a permanence on the one side and a variation on the .other which strangely emphasize and sustain each other, transmitted in endless lines of descent. These lives are not forces, but plastic powers which combine and rule forces, firm yet variable tendencies, purposes which push their way among the fixed laws and the shifting forms of combination which characterize the physical world. These lives even more supersensible than forces, as immediately adaptive and more flexibly adaptive than they, we refer to God as definite powers made distinctly operative among these fixed material conditions. These inner webs of combination we can only understand as the acts of reason, and this fact takes into the Supreme Reason those powers which are the agents of this intricate relationship, daily made to our intellectual vision more complete and beautiful.

To this immediateness of the Supreme Reason expressed in matter and material forces, and yet more expressed in the plastic powers known as life, there will be made strong objection. This relation will be thought not to give the separation between matter and mind which belongs to them, to merge the physical Universe in the Divine Nature, and the Divine Nature in it, in a sort of pantheism. This objection of the religious mind will be sufficiently met in meeting the allied objection of the scientific mind, taken from the opposite side. If the theologian feels that God is too far lost for us in matter, the scientist feels that matter is too far lost for us in God. He will say, We have apparently no true matter, no gross, stubborn qualities that only partially and reluctantly subserve intellectual ends, qualities that bring with them not merely resistance, but inaptness and defilement. This gross substance in my hand or under my foot, preserving its coarse or ugly identity no matter into what undesirable conditions it may have fallen, or what offensive shapes it may have assumed, this cannot be an immediate expression of the divine energy, cannot be here and now the unconstrained divine thought. Matter is apparently an instrument of fixed qualities fairly well adapted to the majority, and perhaps to the most important, of its ends, but often quite unfortunate in its secondary relations and at war with our specific feelings and purposes. We like not to be told, then, that this instrument, so unpliant and defective, instead of being some third thing of mingled good and bad quality between us and God, and seeming to divide the kingdom with him, is the immediate energy of God himself. If this be true, its relatively independent character disappears, its obstinate nature ceases to be a convenient reference of difficulties. We are dealing henceforth directly with God, and must bear over to the Supreme Reason these qualities of our materials, these conditions of our lives, the unfortunate and the fortunate ones alike.

The disposition to regard matter as an independent something casting its limitations upon us, arises from its immediate and gross relations to us, from the remote and supersensual character of our conceptions concerning God, and from the underlying feeling that his action is properly pure, perfect volition, moving directly and unrestrainedly toward its own ends, and not a patient unfolding of principles, the protracted involution and evolution of means and ends.

In a Supreme and completely Rational Nature, the relation of the will to the other powers is very different from that which it sustains in man, whose disproportionate and unsubdued impulses are in constant conflict. With us the right, the holier affections, need to be habitually championed, and their proper champion is the will. Thus will, as personal power, is ever thrusting itself into the foreground, and the good and the evil of the moral world are directly referable to it. Yet will as will is blind impulse, its wholesome service is that which comes to it as the retainer of righteousness, its real character is derived from its relation to the reason. With the Supreme Reason the case is quite different. Will has no separate, no antagonized, existence. It simply underlies as working power a perfectly harmonized and complete nature. The will of God, which we so often and so falsely liken to the will of man, is not pushing personal force, half-blind in its tendencies, it is the quiet on-going of large reason, the simple procedure of a symmetrical and perfectly ordered power, never expressing itself in sudden momentum, in impulses of volition, because there is no resistance within and no resistance without of such magnitude as to provoke and hasten action. Will, then, in God is simply the flow of his rational, beneficent, creative thought, and to expect any portion of his conduct to correspond to those fitful energies in man in which a narrow spirit, and one full of conflicting tendencies, gathers itself up in a convulsive effort, is quite to misunderstand the case. The will of God is the reason of God. In him we are in contact always with a wise, patient—so patient as often to provoke our impatience—purpose, which has complete resources, spread through ample time, at its disposal. The divine thought, therefore, will show no hasty strides of will, called out by hope or fear; no blind pushing power; but the firm unfolding of truth; the steadfast flow of means and ends, each adequate to each; the clear, slow, absolute resolution of all rule into reason.

With this relation in mind of will to reason in the Supreme Reason, by which the one is merely the thoroughly sustained energy of the other, we shall be able better to understand the objection to regarding matter in its properties and laws as the present expression of the activity of God, to wit, that the secondary, instrumental relations of the physical world, so plainly written upon it, are thereby lost. This objection receives its force from our tendency to carry over the human conception of volition to God, and from the supposition that his personal activity, like our own, must always be a direct thrust of will, now in this direction, now in that, among conditions otherwise inert; and one always so rapid and vigorous as to annihilate spaces and times, and to cause means and ends to collapse in instant fulfilment. This is to overlook the supreme under-current of reason, which, by its own nature, spreads out like a river, and maintains its own clear, wholesome, measured flow, merely because that flow is measured, wholesome and clear. If matter were to lose its instrumental character, to cast off and to take on attributes at random, or for transient ends even, it would cease to be the complete expression of reason, and become that of will, arbitrary and fickle human will.

The divine will is rational; it, therefore, tarries in rational dependencies, and gives them full time to do all that was expected of them. In other words, stubborn, slow and faulty an instrument, as in some relations we may think matter to be, it can retain from age to age, and from age to age evolve and enlarge its purely secondary relations, and still be the immediate expression of the Supreme Reason; for reason is ever measuring its forces by its purposes, accepting facts and working by the involution of one relation in another. Reason dwells on this relation of means to ends; on this reciprocal coördination with each other of many parallel lines of activity; on the logical incidents of premises, and the extended causal connections of primary forces and laws, and is satisfied if all is constructively and ultimately shaped to its own purposes. It does not annihilate difficulties, it overcomes them; it does not will order and beauty into being, it thinks them into being, and this even more in their higher than in their lower manifestations.

A third objection to this direct reference of material energies to God seems to us to confront the second or scientific objection of the apparent independence of matter, and, by a mutual balance, to confirm our presentation. It is this: If matter is the direct activity of God, then ought all obstacles, all delays, that arise from it to be directly overcome, either by withdrawing, increasing or modifying its forms, as the case should seem to demand. These two objections spring from the same feeling, and express it in opposite directions. The scientist may say, Matter is stubborn, steadfast, the very antipodes of volition; it *can not* be divine volition. The theologian may say, If matter *is* the divine volition, then ought that volition to break barriers, and push more directly to its ends; it ought not to submit to the endless delays and circumlocutions and failures that physical properties put upon it. Both err from the same feeling; both confuse themselves by supposing volition in its highest as in its lowest forms to be blind, the obliteration of the steps of reason, the instant reaching of ends. The theologian seems ready to say, The reason why the Kingdom of Heaven does not come is because the divine will does not move directly upon its purpose, but chooses, among other things, to allow matter and material conditions to intervene as a retardation, as faulty means to be skilfully worked with, or as a lengthy space-way to be patiently traveled over. The scientist seems ready to say, Matter is plainly a resistance, and often a defeat, to moral ends; it cannot be, therefore, pure divine volition. Both reason most faultily, like Mill, from the premises of infinite power and infinite goodness to the possibility of instant and complete good. All things seem to them open to power, to will. They overlook the fact that reason is the law of the Supreme Reason, that reason assigns to will its conditions, and that will, working otherwise than under these conditions, would be irrational and baffle itself. The theologian and the scientist here incidentally meet on the same ground, and that ground is an oversight of the supremacy of rational relations. The religionist thinks it would be peculiarly divine to annihilate means and ends, and usher in a kingdom with one regal word, to say, Let there be light; and the scientist thinks because means and ends are not so annihilated in the material world, therefore its methods are not spiritual but physical, that matter does not express directly the divine wisdom, but is at best a balance-wheel that sobers down the personal, rational element to a serviceable, practical revolution.

Both scientist and religionist seem to us to fall into a faulty anthropopathic method. The question of the relation of the physical to the spiritual world must be settled by the perfect penetration of the former by the thought, the reason, the relations of the latter. More and more it seems to us to be everywhere interfused with reason, with law, and the fact that these laws, these relations to itself and to man, are not instantly and perfectly gathered up into moral good is incident to the relations themselves, to reason itself—to the fact that extension and time are its very conditions. That they are all working out righteousness is plain, and that they are working it out with such rapidity as reason admits, is becoming more and more plain. The honest objector must here show a better method, not merely assert the possibility of one ; that is to say, he must give reasons, and work in and under reason, and not leap at once beyond it with a *saltus* of pure power or volition. Reason, not power, is the germ of the Universe. To discuss farther the gracious penetration everywhere of matter by mind would be to enter on Natural Theology, and this is not our purpose ; we only wish to indicate some reasons for regarding the physical world as the immediate, instant outcome of the Divine Mind.

This view assigns to matter and to mind their true relations. Matter is not thus something alien to mind, imposing its own difficulties on the otherwise quick and skilful thoughts ; matter in its properties and dependencies is purely the product of mind, is rational from beginning to end, and from side to side, is the mind's immediate form of activity, its speech. Tardy and defective developments are not due to matter but to mind, are, in the widest scope of reason, not so much real as apparent.

Matter is nothing and does nothing except as the ground of its being and doing are given it. Difficulties are not in matter as something inert, an obstacle in the path of reason, they are in reason itself. Reason in all its activities by its very nature sets up connections, relations, limitations; and what it has set up it cannot without reason, that is, without other limitations and relations, pull down again. There is not, then, a property in matter which is not rationally there, and which must not, therefore, remain there, till a sufficient reason appears for its removal. The laws of reason are emphatically *laws*, indeed the only laws, and it does not belong to any volition, not even the divine volition, to rush by them, or confound them in a *coup de main*. Grant that the law of inheritance may produce a monster, the monster is so far forth a rational product, demanded by conditions broadly and constructively operative, and we cannot wisely ask such results to be anticipated by an intervention of will, or in shamefacedness ascribe them to the awkward and clumsy ways of Nature *versus* God. Reason is the primary nature, the eternal constructive nature, which gives its laws to all things as they flow from it. The wisdom of God cannot be saved by an apology based on the difficulties it encounters. If the physical constitution of the world does not seem to us to be rational, it is not because the divine reason is not everywhere in it, in the calm, clear flow of a perennial purpose; but because we have not insight, experience and scope enough fully to discern that divine thought. Our growing knowledge has taught us a thousand times the deeper lessons, the truer significance, of physical laws; and will till the very end, till matter, like a transparent crystal without a flaw, shall let the light of the divine mind completely through it. Surely as we have waited not in vain hitherto, we may well preserve a little longer this waiting attitude.

The relation now suggested between nature and God best accords with our own experience. In some inscrutable way we do put our thought and energy into the work of our hands. The engineer with his engine turns the sudden purpose of his mind into immediate movement and ponderous force. The musician with his instrument converts feelings into pulsations of air, that occupy and delight the sense of hearing with the same positive being as do the waves of a dancing lake the vision. We feel and we act in every part of our bodies, yet we are not these bodies. We, indeed, create no forces, but we use and direct them, an act of sovereignty of the same intellectual scope. We may liken God's relation to the Universe to this connection, so intimate to us, of our bodies and our minds, and this familiar yet inscrutable dependence may shadow forth the invisible things of God. That the image only touches and does not cover the case is a matter of course. If it were more exact, it would destroy itself by a too complete correspondence.

A third fitness which belongs to this view is the harmony it establishes between the natural and the supernatural. We can reject neither; certainly not the natural, unless our reason is to grow giddy again in an aimless whirl of appearances, in the inconstant fears of superstition; certainly not the supernatural, unless our reason in all its hopes and affections is to be frozen up by laws that bind, but bind for no benignant purpose; in forces that creep forward, but creep forward with no more freedom and no more beneficence than the grinding glacier. But if we are to hold both the natural and the supernatural, the well-defined method and the internal power, the means by which and the energy with which thought works, then both must be in harmony, amenable to the same Supreme Reason. The natural cannot be one set of forces governed by one principle, and the supernatural be a second set controlled by a conflicting principle. Under the view now offered it is one divine energy in the natural and supernatural that flows forward, or bends on either hand, according to the permanent and the shifting conditions of reason. Reason is the most permanent, the most pliant of all powers, of all processes. It is not a machine, though it can work with its inflexible energy; it is not a fortuitous force, though it has all the flexibility of freedom, though like the fluent air, it feels everywhere the heat, the heat of the least affection or colliding impulse in the human heart.

We thus gather up in this view all that either science or theology can teach us. We meet God as the scientist would have us meet him, in nature and under the laws of nature; and we meet him as the theologian would have us meet him, as the Supreme Presence and Ruler in the world. Neither branch is sacrificed, the physical and the personal, the fixed and the flexible, the form and the spirit, are firmly held and indissolubly blended. We are not allowed to wander dreamily in our work and our thought, for here is nature, God with *us;* we are not allowed to grovel in our labor, or be indolent in it, or despair of it, for here is Revelation, *God* with us.

There is one other weighty confirmation. These relations of matter and mind make the connection of God with his work one and the same for all time ; whatever God has been, that he is ; and what he is not to-day, that he has never been. Homogeneity of relationship, uniformity of method, these are the very pith of omniscience, omnipotence, omnipresence. Any theory of the Universe that puts God here and now outside its bounds as far as creation or control or intervention are concerned, and, then, by compensation relegates the divine wisdom and power to some point of beginning, where he was all in all, is self-destructive. The principles and fundamental relations that prevail once prevail always. There may be, there must be, minor changes within the development, the unfolding itself ; changes giving modifications of method, but the fundamental relations of matter and mind, of the Universe with its Author, cannot be of this order. There can be in the moral even less than in the physical world extended cataclysms. The thought and power of God are pervasive, or they have no existence. If we set apart times and places for them, they will soon vanish altogether.

If this Universe can lie unsustained in the present, if it can hold possession of the æons of evolution, we need no God simply to give the thoughts a fictitious beginning, a start-off. But perfect support in this Universe of living energies can only mean perpetual creation; to mean less is to mean nothing. If the forces in the world are now sufficient unto themselves, they were so a year since, two years since, in all past time. In what one moment and by what sudden change do they, as we trace them back through the flow of time, lose independence and become dependent. There is no homogeneity in such a conception, and we have in it two inscrutable things instead of one, and then an inscrutable relation between them. The imagination may play many tricks with us in distant periods, but time itself comes forward with a terrible identity of relations, a sublime homogeneity of methods.

The conception of God is of little worth to us, would be practically lost, under such a transfer of his power to an act of creation. We are now thoroughly enclosed by physical forces, and if we venture on the past or on the future these same conditions encompass us everywhere, and cradle the race as the ocean the ships that rest on its bosom. A Supernatural, a Divinity beyond the bounds of the Universe, if such things are, have no more relation to life than lunar measurements to a land speculator. They bring us no duties, raise no hopes, offer no consolations.

The Supreme Reason is supreme in every

moment and every place and every action. This
is the only external fact properly correlative with
the rational conception. The homogeneity of the
Divine Life is the first term in its apprehension,
not a dead but a living homogeneity, not a statical
but a dynamical one. That we live and move and
have our being in God, is the crowning truth of
reason and Revelation.

In what we have now said of the Supreme
Reason, we have not so much defined the conception, outlined it, as erased the outlines that our too
eager thoughts had given it, and so guarded ourselves against its perversion. Yet is not this great
area of the infinite empty. It is an overflowing
centre rather than a visible circumference. It contains all we see and know and vaguely catch at, as
the heavens hold suns and planets in ample depths
with no limits and no plethora. Seeing something
of that little orb of life in which we play a part, we
have yet vision enough left to look out into the infinite spaces of being about us, to contrast the finite
reason with the Supreme Reason which envelops
it everywhere. As we see reason traveling downward to reach and include the lowest physical relations, so also, moving upward in thought along
these same connections, we meet with the conditions of consciousness, then with consciousness,
then with an enlarging intellectual experience in
the world, then with a rational comprehension of
that experience, then with a spiritual kingdom,
enclosing all, and so pass onward by every grade
of intelligence to the Supreme Reason, the Source

of All. The physical creation thus contains and reflects the spiritual world, till in man the response between them becomes complete, and, like the images multiplied between two opposed mirrors, he is taken into the heart of both. Not only does the light greet everything in the world, every coarsest thing in the world selects from it a color, and so marshals itself in its festive troop. Each thing under the higher play of Reason has a reason of its own, and so stands up together with the works of God.

THE END.

INDEX.

---

www.ingramcontent.com/pod-product-compliance
Lightning Source LLC
Chambersburg PA
CBHW031406270326
41929CB00010BA/1347